Outsourcing IT – The Legal Aspects

Outsourcing IT – The Legal Aspects

Planning, Contracting, Managing and the Law

Second Edition

RACHEL BURNETT

GOWER

Published by
Gower Publishing Limited
Wey Court East
Union Road
Farnham
Surrey GU9 7PT
England

Ashgate Publishing Company
Suite 420
101 Cherry Street
Burlington, VT 05401-4405
USA

Rachel Burnett has asserted her moral right under the Copyright, Designs and Patents Act, 1988, to be identified as the author of this work.

www.gowerpublishing.com

British Library Cataloguing in Publication Data
Burnett, Rachel
   Outsourcing IT : the legal aspects : planning, contracting, managing and the law
   1. Computer contracts - Great Britain
   I. Title
   343.7'30999

   ISBN-13: 978-0-566-08597-0

Library of Congress Cataloging-in-Publication Data
Burnett, Rachel.
   Outsourcing IT : the legal aspects : planning, contracting, managing and the law / by Rachel Burnett.
   -- 2nd ed.
     p. cm.
   Includes bibliographical references and index.
   ISBN 978-0-566-08597-0
   1. Computer contracts--Great Britain. 2. Contracting out--Great Britain. 3. Information technology--Great Britain. 4. Computer contracts. 5. Contracting out. 6. Information technology. I. Title.
   KD1642.C65B87 2009
   343.41'07--dc22

                                                                                          2008042765

Mixed Sources
Product group from well-managed forests and other controlled sources
www.fsc.org Cert no. SGS-COC-2482
© 1996 Forest Stewardship Council

Printed and bound in Great Britain by
TJ International Ltd, Padstow, Cornwall.

Contents

Foreword to the Second Edition

Coming from a background in the chemical industry, I have always been a little puzzled at the continuing intensity of the debate on outsourcing in the IT industry.

In the older (and maturer) of the two industries, product value chains divide naturally between focused and specialized providers – on the one hand the manufacturers of the major volume commodities, on the other hand the manufacturers of more specialized products. And the issue of offshoring? Well, globalization of manufacturing has become the norm with tariff liberalization since the 1950's – over 50 per cent of global commerce in manufacturing is now traded internationally, and nowhere more so than in the chemical industry.

The younger IT industry is still early on its learning curve. Its hardware-manufacturing sector behaves a lot like the chemical industry – but its data processing and storage, software and services sectors, very differently. The technical architectures that still rule at the heart of legacy systems predicate tightly integrated systems, tightly coupled processes – a delight to the great phalanx of suppliers, including systems integrators, whose 'bums on seats' business models thrive on the multiplication of the deep expertise required endlessly to unravel and re-weave the consequent inter-dependent complexities.

So, as the economic benefits of focus and specialization have encouraged the development of IT outsourcing 'along the value chain', it is the lawyers who have led the way in developing and articulating a major body of learning in how best to deliver success; how best to manage risk; how best to set the foundations on which, possibly, something approaching an effective business partnership might slowly develop.

This second edition of Rachel Burnett's seriously practical *vade mecum* of outsourcing is thus to be welcomed – the classic guide to tackling the challenging complexities of an effective outsourcing deal. Here is the lawyer as pedagogue

– in no way pedantic or dogmatic, but clear in her explanations and rich in her illustrations.

Early in the book, Rachel reviews the processes by which the choice of potential suppliers is made, putting a particular emphasis on the importance of this task. The ever accelerating tick-tock of the Moore's Law clock endlessly shifts the underlay of the enabling technologies that IT suppliers exploit – and so also the balance of factors that scope the business models they pursue. Newer suppliers enter the market exploiting new business models (Google, as an example, with its highly commoditized outsourcing offer in the 'search' business process space – arguably now the largest global BPO supplier). Supplier selection is one key fulcrum in building effective outsourcing leverage.

In parallel, Rachel's chapter on services and service level agreements scopes the lines of attack that allow the complexities that lie at the multiple points of engagement between customer and suppler to be disciplined and properly positioned for effective risk management – and the acid test, the second key fulcrum, of a quality outsourcing contract lies in its ability to deliver processes of risk management that outlive the contract itself.

A young industry working hard to climb a steep learning curve – and Rachel admirably revisits again and again the vital role of the human contribution in both shaping the deal and in managing it effectively thereafter. The British Computer Society (BCS), of which Rachel was President 2007–2008, has been a leader in redefining the range of skills that the modern Chartered IT Professional (CITP) requires – and in parallel more specialized associations have followed that lead – such as the International Association of Outsourcing Professionals (IAOP) with the Chartered Outsourcing Professional (COP). Lawyers such as Rachel deliver the benefits of deeply rooted traditions of professionalism to an industry just starting to awake to its benefits – and her book sits at the nexus of this vitally needed transformation.

So, as both putative customer and putative supplier work to create an outsourcing relationship that will sustainably work, and sustainably deliver the business objectives of both, here is the homework that both must first digest and then diligently apply. It is the price that our young industry has to pay until, one day, it finally unravels its endless complexities and can behave a little more like its older and more experienced peers!

Dr Richard Sykes FRSA
(Chairman, Outsourcing and Offshore Group, Intellect)

Foreword to the First Edition

From one point of view 'outsourcing' information systems and technology is little more than another name for a well-established practice. No commercial computer users have designed and built their own computers since Lyons built Lyons Electronic Office (LEO) for their famous Tea Shop system more than 40 years ago. What we now call 'outsourcing' is on one analysis just a continuation of a trend.

What makes outsourcing in the sense used in this book so different and so complex? To a professional information systems practitioner several features stand out.

One is the large number of eggs in one basket. The tendency to bundle the development of systems and/or the provision of software with the operation and updating of a service exposes customers to peculiar potential risks.

Another is the risk of being locked into indefinite dependence on a supplier, even when the original contract has run its course, and the difficulty of changing suppliers if the service is poor or the relationship has broken down.

Yet another is the comprehensive and complex nature of the deal. The ideal of a contract whose terms unambiguously anticipate and provide for every conceivable eventuality is totally unrealistic for transactions of this kind. Differences in expectations, understanding and interpretation between the parties will inevitably occur. The trick is to have a means of resolving them before they develop into disputes.

To compound all that, the deal may deprive customers of direct control over their information systems strategy in support of their business, and leave them without access to the professional competences needed to manage and negotiate with suppliers.

All these issues, and others which must not be ignored, such as intellectual property arrangements, the complexities of transferring staff, property and other assets, tendering procedures and performance monitoring are addressed in this book.

Its scope is rather modestly expressed as the key factors involved in the legal agreement. In fact the prospective agreement forms the focus to identify and discuss a comprehensive range of topics with a degree of insight which is music to the ears of an information systems engineer.

No-one who is not prepared to think hard about and think through all the issues raised in this book should contemplate outsourcing IT. Thinking them through and collecting and analysing all the data they demand will, however, be a most beneficial exercise for any organization, even if it does not after all proceed with outsourcing.

The advice in this book should be welcomed by suppliers too, as counterparties to outsourcing contracts. Well planned and well structured outsourced assignments, from well-informed and well advised customers, are much more likely to be satisfactory to suppliers.

It is clear from Rachel Burnett's comprehensive treatment of this topic that the parties to outsourcing contracts need access to very well informed and competent legal advice. I believe it also becomes clear that in many cases the creation and subsequent operation of these contracts requires reliance on support analogous to the role of the independent consulting engineer in other fields, to ensure smooth and fair operation, to facilitate the rapid resolution of differences and to provide a means of managing the changes and evolutionary developments which are inescapable in such a dynamic field of endeavour.

This book lays an excellent foundation for an understanding of how to progress to successful outsourcing and none of its contents can safely be disregarded.

Ron McQuaker
Exxel Consultants Limited
(Past President of the British Computer Society 1996–7)

Preface to the Second Edition

Outsourcing has increased in popularity and evolved in various styles to various degrees of sophistication since the first edition of this book was published. The second edition of this book, as the first, is a guide to the principal features which should be considered in drawing up and managing contracts for outsourcing information technology (IT) and information systems. Its purpose is to help business managers to understand the key factors involved in the legal agreement, both for organizations which are considering outsourcing and for organizations which provide outsourcing.

The basic principles have not changed significantly since the first edition, although there have been legal and commercial developments over the last ten years, in the areas particularly of public procurement, data protection and human resources – and offshoring.

A legal contract should set out what has been agreed between the parties, covering all the elements of the arrangements which matter. It should never be treated as something separate and unrelated to business reality which is signed for respectability and subsequently ignored. The negotiation of the details of the terms may well raise matters which had not initially been thought about. The resulting decisions will benefit the long term relationship of the supplier and customer in clarifying the nature of the arrangements and promoting the commercial success of the transaction.

I hope that I have made the main legal issues associated with outsourcing accessible to readers who may never have had to consider them before, and that I have reinforced the message for those readers for whom outsourcing is a more familiar subject.

As this is intended to be a practical book for IT managers, references to statutes or case law are made only as appropriate to indicate sources where this might be useful, not to give authority for every statement as would be done for an academic text.

It should also be noted that the discussions in the book proceed on the basis of the legal jurisdiction of England and Wales.

Rachel Burnett

Introduction

The last two decades have witnessed a significant trend towards ever-increasing outsourcing by firms in most developed economies. This trend reverses an earlier pattern in the evolution and growth of large industrial firms towards greater levels of vertical integration that prevailed during most of the previous 100 years.[1]

Moreover, over the last twenty or so years, outsourcing has developed immensely in scope, sophistication and ambition. This book focuses on information technology (IT) outsourcing, which is potentially more complex than other outsourcing. It therefore covers what is generally applicable to all outsourcing, as well as focusing on what is specifically relevant for IT.

There is now much information available from the experience of those involved and their advisers, from both commercial and academic research and theories, analyses and statistics, to learn how to overcome the problems which arose from the unbridled enthusiasm and careless, even reckless, lack of foresight evident in some of the early pioneering outsourcing deals – and indeed many since then – which attempted to control the surging costs and uncertain quality of part or all of their IT equipment, systems and services.

One of the most important lessons is that a good contract, where time has been spent on developing a strategy and effort has been devoted to negotiating it, will obviate many of the potential unforeseen costs and other risks otherwise inherent in the relationship. Through the contract a customer will assert responsibility for its non-delegable obligations, and avoid consequent loss of control of the function or process being outsourced. The parties' respective roles will be clarified. The services and their service levels will be properly defined as will the charging rates and formulae. The duration of the relationship will be specified.

---

1   'Research on Outsourcing: Theoretical Perspectives and Empirical Evidence', K. Matthew Gilley, Abdul A. Rasheed and Hussam Al Shammari, in *Global Outsourcing Strategies*, Ed. Peter Barrar and Roxane Gervais, Gower 2006.

Commentators on outsourcing all emphasise the importance of the contract in the outsourcing transaction. It is likely to be a complicated and intricate document to draft and negotiate, unique for the particular circumstances, having precise and objective criteria for measuring what is to be delivered and paid for. It should benefit both parties. Managers in organizations paying for outsourcing, and in businesses offering outsourcing, should be fully conversant with the scope and the essential details of the transaction which has been agreed, by means of a contract which will help them in working together to make the arrangement a success.

Definitions

The terms 'supplier' and 'customer' are used throughout this book, for consistency and simplicity, to identify respectively the company providing the outsourcing services and the company or other organization paying for the services. Other terms frequently used in practice are 'vendor' or 'provider' for the former and 'client' or 'user' for the latter. 'Transferor' and 'transferee' are used in Chapter 6 dealing with human resources, and in particular the implications of the law relating to transfer of staff from customer to supplier.

The term 'outsourcing' is taken to mean that defined activities, or services, are contracted out by a customer to a supplier to manage and run to agreed standards over an agreed period of time. It may encompass the transfer to the supplier of the customer's staff and/or fixed assets and/or premises used in the provision of the services. 'Management' and 'agreed standards' are the important words. It is more than the provision of specialist skills in limited supply for a defined purpose, or resources for a specific project, or where the arrangement is simply for support and maintenance by a third party. It is not merely procurement. Contractual commitments to service levels are integral to the arrangements. It is a development of 'facilities management'. Although the latter is about a facility, process or service run externally by a third party for the customer organization, little control of management or service levels is required.

Trends

Expenditure on outsourcing continues to increase in most developed economies, including the UK, which outsources more than any other European country. Outsourcing as a phenomenon continues to evolve, and different and varied functions and services are candidates for outsourcing. The number of contracts continues to grow, but there are fewer high value long term contracts.

The market is maturing, and attitudes to outsourcing have changed. Early unalloyed and uncritical commitment by naïve customers has given place to some disillusion and cynicism in a turbulent business environment. It is not unusual for outsourced systems or functions to be brought back in-house once an outsourcing contract has come to an end, whether by expiry or early termination – by either the customer or the supplier. For example, Sainsbury's terminated its IT transformation outsourcing, valued in 2003 at over £2 billion.[2] JP Morgan Chase's seven-year $5 billion contract with IBM in 2002 was cancelled two years later.[3] The outsourcing was of the IT services infrastructure, including data centres, help desks, data and voice networks, together with the transfer of 4,000 employees. In 2004 the bank merged with Bank One, and brought the IT infrastructure and the employees back in-house. The new management considered that this was a critical move to gain competitive advantage.

Many customers are on the third or fourth wave of outsourcing, and consequently have much more experience in negotiating contracts and in evaluating innovative proposals, and suppliers now specialise in markets or technologies. Business process outsourcing and transformational outsourcing have become more popular and are better defined.

IT itself is affecting outsourcing. Persistent technology standardization means that customers are not tied down to a very limited number of suppliers, and are better able to drive a bargain. At the same time, new technologies, such as virtualization, standardization and systems automation, facilitate effective economics of scale.

There are more and more expert and specialist sources of advice available for guidance at every stage. There are advisers in the cultural implications of particular offshore countries, consultants to recommend courses of action for transition management, and standards professionals to help with benchmarking at defined stages of the contract term.

IT has become part of the modern process of globalization, with offshoring now an acknowledged route for cost savings and productivity gains. Along with other industries, the financial services sector has moved much of its work

---

2   Reported in *Computing*, 10 November 2005.
3   Reported at http://www.silicon.com/research/specialreports/enterprise/0,3800003425,39124018,00.
     htm.

offshore, starting with high volume routine work such as call centres and data processing, but now extended beyond this level to higher value operations and transformation services. Business process outsourcing is growing fastest.

The development of outsourcing

For over a hundred years, companies organised their productive activities by integrating them internally. The archetypal example is the mass production of Ford cars at the Dearborn plant in Michigan. Iron ore, coal, sand and rubber were input, and Model T Fords were output.

Forty years ago when only the biggest, most forward looking companies and parts of the public sector were investing in computers, they owned the machines and employed cohorts of analysts and programmers. The large stand-alone mainframes took up vast areas of load-bearing floor space, used for automatic processing of massive volumes of data. The important contracts in data processing were for the purchase of hardware from the computer suppliers. The basic software to run the machines arrived 'bundled' with them. Almost all application systems for these companies comprised suites of program individually designed and coded, including those routines needed for every system, such as sorting and printing; whether the systems were for number-crunching, for other office activities, or were specially devised for a company's unique requirements.

It has always been common practice for a business to commission external contractors to assist with IT analysis and programming. Large companies might give themselves some flexibility in recruiting temporary staff, where they were unsure of their ongoing work volumes or where they needed additional specialist expertise. Smaller companies who were unable to justify the capital investment to create their own computing facilities, and other companies of all sizes who saw no need for major capital IT investment, used external bureau services. Contracts for the work to be done by independent contractors, or by bureaux, would therefore centre on the operational computer system being run, or the number of resources required, or the hours individually worked.

As the functions of the departments responsible for computing were transformed from processing reams of data into managing information technology, it continued to be difficult to get sufficient permanent in-house expertise. The development of new systems and the acquisition of novel technology were risky undertakings, with constant shortages of skilled and experienced resources. The mainframe bureau service and the supply of contractors and programming resources adapted. Software houses, system integrators and management consultancies expanded, undertaking software development, providing services as required, and agreeing to run the implemented systems. Third party maintenance and support services grew. The use of external resources became a cost effective way of keeping a company's moribund machines going, or of managing legacy systems.

In the 1980s the political doctrine of privatising public sector services began to be put into effect. Government shareholdings in private businesses such as Jaguar and BP were sold. The process continued with the privatization of state-owned businesses like BT and the utilities.

In the public sector, policy making was separated from the executive functions of the Civil Service. Agencies were created and market testing programmes were formulated for contracting out different kinds of services.

Gradually in both public and private sectors more services were sent outside, including management tasks, and closely defined results began to be demanded. Services had to add value for the customer. Ultimately this could extend to the whole IT and management services departments. Assets and staff being used to provide services in-house would be transferred to the supplier and the services bought back, the supplier using its own assets and staff. Outsourcing had thus become strategic and its methodology refined, covering a range of services, processes and industries.

The high risk 100 per cent outsourcings of entire IT departments or major functions of blue chip companies or public sector departments always hit the headlines. They were therefore perceived to be typical, although in fact they were newsworthy because they were unusual. A number of them also gained publicity when they came to an untimely end, sometimes not long after the contract started, sometimes much later. Some ran their full term, but at a far higher cost than envisaged, taking account of major business changes. For example, all the Inland Revenue's IT operations were privatised in 1994 with many fanfares, to EDS at an original estimate of one billion pounds over ten years, in combination with the system development of the major tax reform of self assessment. Over the term the costs increased vastly. In 2003 after a procurement process of nearly two years, the Inland Revenue entered into a new ten-year contract, valued at £3 billion a year, with Cap Gemini Ernst & Young and its partner Fujitsu Services, to develop the technology platform as well as support and maintenance.

However, most outsourcing is selective, with customers using a combination of options, and the risks are much lower. The simplest kind of contract is for commodity outsourcing, where services are repetitive and routine. It is easy to compare suppliers, and costs may be fixed. Moving up from this, selective outsourcing options may be for a variety of IT management functions and processes: technical services, networks, data centres, help desks. A supplier may manage the customer's applications and be responsible for further systems development.

Conventional wisdom was to avoid outsourcing core activities, although the definition of 'core activities' differs even within the same industry from company to company. Now with transformational outsourcing, the external supplier implements programmes intended to drive business performance change fundamentally for the customer's IT, business models and related risks. This goes to the heart of the customer's business, the supplier providing the leadership and strategic agenda to improve performance by rapid and radical engineered change, perhaps to market position, or even through diversification.

Meanwhile IT-related contract formats and contents have been changing in order to accommodate these developing business practices. It is essential to have contract provisions which are appropriate for the kinds of outsourcing services being supplied.

The decision to outsource

Business conditions change and great care needs to be taken in evaluating the risks of outsourcing IT and information systems activities of long term significance: such activities as strategic planning; information resource management; decision support systems; strategic applications planning and business analysis. The risk must be minimized of the customer inadvertently abandoning control of a key resource to external suppliers.

In these circumstances, the customer should be asking itself questions about its business objectives and philosophy in order to justify its decision on outsourcing; for example:

- Is the IT strategy and operation in a state which is stable, measurable and suitable for contracting out? Outsourcing a problem is no solution.

- How will outsourcing fit in with the overall business direction?

- What benefits are being sought? Are these realistic?

- Might security be compromised?

- How will success be measured?

- Where will innovation, whether technological or in information systems, originate?

The decision to outsource should be taken for sound business reasons. It should not be driven by technological considerations nor by costs savings alone. Even if financial reasons may lie behind the move to outsourcing, they should not be the sole long term objective.

Yet in many companies, the directors see IT and its associated services as a high cost and risk, and a major frustration in practice. Attracting and retaining good quality experienced IT staff is a problem, and staff costs are high. In spite of falling technology prices, distributed processing and downsizing generally, the costs never seem to come down sufficiently. New system requirements, constant technological innovation and continuous adaptation of software by modifications, enhancements and upgrades, ensure that change is endemic.

With outsourcing the move may be made from fixed but increasing internal costs to costs which can be negotiated in advance with competing suppliers and risks shared. These costs may initially appear to be less expensive. They will be assessed differently from the calculation of the costs of running IT in-house, and they may consequently seem to be more acceptable by offering more certainty in their rates and greater flexibility in the choice of what to pay for. Outsourcing is therefore often perceived by a Board of Directors as being an immediate route to operational cost savings, a superficially attractive argument which is not necessarily justifiable in the long term. Decisions on outsourcing should always take the quality of service into account along with any perceived savings, over the expected life time of the outsourced activity.

Positive reasons for outsourcing are:

- To limit uncertainties by predicting costs (where this is feasible).

- To focus in-house resources on more strategic business issues or on new technology and systems.

- To reduce IT management time spent on recruitment, budgeting, administration, selection of technology.

- To gain access to new technologies and skills – perhaps on the basis of economies of scale, in that suppliers can acquire the latest technology by spreading the costs over a number of customers, whereas it can be difficult for an individual customer to justify the continuous application of up-to-date technology for itself.

- To improve business efficiency, by buying in a more systematic approach to service provision.

Surveys show that while cost savings can be achieved, services outsourced can easily cost more than those retained in-house. For instance, one study by Gartner found that the cost increased on average by nearly a third. The hidden costs of outsourcing, such as contract management support, had not been taken into account. There was also a risk in outsourcing customer-facing operations merely as a cost-cutting exercise. The research showed that costs will not fall, and dissatisfied customers will be lost.[4] A more recent study by Deloitte[5] found that customers were achieving anticipated cost savings, but were losing opportunities to innovate. They were disappointed because they had not understood what the outsourcing could bring and had not planned for it sufficiently well. They had limited their focus to cost reduction objectives rather than considering a business case for efficiency strategies or transformation of their operations.

The legal context

The law which applies to the IT outsourcing services contract is principally the law applicable to IT contracts generally. The contract is also largely affected by corporate law, and the laws of intellectual property, confidentiality and data protection. For the UK, as for other member states of the European Union (EU), legislation from the EU incorporated into English law with the overall objective of achieving an open market, is also especially relevant in relation to the procurement of services in the public sector, the subject of Chapter 3, and about the transfer of staff, discussed in Chapter 6.

---

4   Reported at http://news.zdnet.co.uk/itmanagement/0,1000000308,39190514,00.htm.
5   'Why Settle for Less', reported at http://www.reuters.com/article/pressRelease/idUS221212+14-Feb-2008+PRN20080214.

Structure of the book

The chapters which follow each concentrate on different aspects of the IT outsourcing contract.

The structure and format of the contract are discussed at Chapter 1. The planning for outsourcing and the time scale allowed must allow time for contract drafting and negotiating. It is easy to underestimate the level of detail to be taken into account when decisions have to be taken.

The customer's choice of supplier should be made carefully. This is the theme of Chapter 2. The expertise may exist in-house or outsourcing consultants may be appointed to advise, often co-ordinated as part of a team to represent the different interests. At the early stages, the selection processes may be highly confidential. There should be a defined, objective procedure for the selection, and the criteria will include the supplier's financial stability, experience, quality provision, compatibility and flexibility. Multiple suppliers may be considered, although challenges will arise for the customer in managing more than one supplier.

The selection process for central government, utilities and local authorities is formalised under the public procurement regime and compulsory competitive tendering, as explained at Chapter 3.

Chapter 4 focuses on services and service level agreements, the heart of the contractual relationship, the most important and yet the most difficult part to formulate correctly.

The transfer of the customer's business assets of equipment and premises may form part of the outsourcing transaction, outlined in Chapter 5. A complex area of law has developed and continues to evolve in respect of transfer of staff, driven by European legislation, which cannot be ignored and is explained in Chapter 6.

In most IT contracts, software and other intellectual property must be correctly licensed or the ownership transferred, discussed in Chapter 7. For outsourcing, the supplier must be able to run software originally licensed to the customer by third parties. The supplier's use of its own software may cause particular concerns long term.

Chapter 8 identifies a number of ways in which the charges for the outsourcing services may be calculated.

Once outsourcing is an accomplished fact, the customer's IT management roles must be adapted. No longer will there be responsibility for running the IT function which has been outsourced, but there will be management control in order to ensure that the outsourcing arrangement is effective in practice. The customer should no more be able to walk away from the outsourcing of its IT function than it would be able to distance itself entirely from any other important part of its business. Outsourcing failure or success will depend on effective management by the customer, and on successful liaison between customer and supplier. Co-operation and good will, so essential to IT management generally, are vital to outsourcing contracts, but not at the expense of having proper control procedures and objective measurements. Chapter 9 proposes procedures for liaison, which should be set out in the contract. Formal methods for variations to the contract requirements are part of this liaison, as recommended in Chapter 10.

In Chapter 11 the issues of confidentiality, security and reliability are discussed. These will differ in importance from system to system and from customer to customer. Whatever is involved in the particular transaction must be identified and specified in the contract.

The contract will last for a fixed period of time. In negotiating the contract there is often a perception of permanence. Having taken the decision to outsource and to negotiate the desired conditions for the long term, the customer may often perceive the new process and relationship to be effectively permanent. Nevertheless, there is always the possibility of the relationship coming to an end at some time in the future, whether through the breakdown of the association over time, a clash of management personalities, the financial vulnerability of the outsourcing supplier, a change of business direction on the part of either party, or for other reasons. Chapter 12 describes the options open to the customer, whether the choice is to be contract renewal, a new contract with another supplier or bringing the services back in-house. The consequences must be set out in the contract, so that it is clear what the responsibilities of each party are.

It is essential always to bear in mind for any negotiations what the fundamental requirements are, what the objective is to be, and to have enforceability and dispute management terms set out in the contract as a practical back stop should any aspect of the transaction go badly wrong. The supplier must limit its liability realistically. The customer will expect some remedies to be available if things do go wrong. This is the subject of Chapter 13.

Chapter 14 is an introduction to offshore outsourcing. Chapter 15 concludes by giving an example of an outline contract framework and provides reference information.

Contract Planning, Structuring and Negotiating

Surveys on successes and failures of outsourcing consistently emphasize that satisfied customers had signed comprehensive contracts where the issues had been thought through, and dissatisfied customers had not signed contracts which were clear or detailed. Whether as a supplier or as a customer, it is vital to have a properly negotiated contract in writing with the other party to the outsourcing arrangements, covering legal, commercial and service requirements.

In this chapter, some points relating to the contract structure are examined. These include the planning necessary before starting to draft the wording, the decisions on the resources to use, the framework for the contents, the philosophy behind it, the law which should apply, and other basic formalities.

Broadly, the contract will cover, amongst other things, the services to be provided, the charges, the rights and responsibilities of each side, the management of the contract, the extent of the parties' liabilities, how variations to the services may be made and how the contract may be brought to an end. There may be separate documents for the transfer of assets or the business, for staff transfer, and for the services agreements.

Because the outsourcing arrangement relates to one particular business and organization and to carefully defined services to be supplied, the contract – which may consist of a series of linked documents – must be tailor-made.

The reasons for having a contract

There are at least three good reasons for formal terms to be drawn up and agreed.

The first is that the contract framework will also serve as a structure for the negotiating process. This will guide discussion on all the matters to be covered and eventually help consensus to be reached, so that both parties to the contract understand exactly what it is they are agreeing, unambiguously.

The second is that the contract should be a source of reference during the provision of the outsourcing services. The contract will serve as a working document, detailing information about what has been agreed, such as the charging methods or the reporting procedure, or the benchmarks for measuring the service levels which are achieved in practice.

Thirdly, however amicable and trusting the apparent relationship between the parties at the outset, the individuals involved in negotiating the contract cannot be regarded as permanent fixtures over the course of the outsourcing. The supplier will have a number of staff working day-to-day on the contract who will not have been concerned in the contract negotiation and who may vary over time. The managers and representatives of either party may be promoted, retire, change role or move organization. The directors of each party may decide on a new strategy for their business one or two or five years hence. For all these reasons and more, the contract should, in common with all contracts, set out each party's respective rights and responsibilities clearly, so that in the final analysis the contract can be enforced if any of the important obligations fail to be carried out and the relationship deteriorates. For both parties, the objectives of what they are trying to achieve from entering into an agreement for outsourcing need always to be borne in mind. A successful outsourcing contract should accurately reflect in its detail the context of the unique relationship between the supplier and the customer for the purposes of the business objectives of the outsourcing. In other words, the contract document must accurately reflect the individual components of the transaction which the parties believe they have made. This will involve close attention to both operational and technical matters. However, it will be negotiated under the pressures of a deadline where solutions to different perspectives and opinions must be agreed, and under these constraints, it will never be perfect.

The parties to the contract

Who are the parties to the contract to be? A contract must be between legal entities to be enforceable. Corporations, the majority of which are companies formed under the Companies Acts, and charities, which are companies subject to special regulations, are entitled to make contracts. The Crown and other emanations of the State such as Government departments may enter into contracts, as may local authorities. Organizations set up under other statutes – some quasi-public Commissions would fall under this heading – are able to exist legally according to what they are permitted to do under the statute concerned, which would normally allow contracts to be made by them. Individuals and partnerships are also legal persons.

A holding company, as shareholder of its subsidiary company, is under English company law a separate legal entity from it, and cannot, simply because of that relationship, speak for the subsidiary or enter into contracts on the subsidiary's behalf. Similarly the subsidiary has no legal obligation to act as directed by the holding company. On the contrary, the directors of the subsidiary are required to consider its interests independently and may incur personal liability if they fail to do so.

It sometimes happens that either the supplier or the customer may regard itself as a self-contained organization, yet be without any distinct legal identity of its own, being in fact merely an operating division within a company. The contract should then be entered into by the main corporate body itself, which will be the party legally responsible. A statement at the start of the contract can make it clear that the contract is between 'X Company Limited' and 'Headco plc by its Systems Division'. In the body of the contract, the company may be referred to by the abbreviated version of the name with which everyone is familiar, such as 'Systems', or the name by which the division or department is known, if this will make the contract more user friendly and the rights and obligations more readily comprehensible.

Provided that all the terms have been agreed, it is not essential under English law for most contracts to be signed. However, there may be operating rules for the supplier or customer organization about entering into contracts, and if one of the parties is an organization established under the laws of another jurisdiction, it will have to abide by the legislation applicable to its formation and operation. In any event, it is good business practice to record formally the commitment of each party to the agreement that has been reached, signifying the conclusion of the negotiations. Indeed, the event of signing the contract is often marked as a special occasion with suitable publicity arrangements, photographs taken to record the cordial handshakes, the press release issued, and the first cheque handed over.

The contract should therefore be signed by representatives with the authority to do so, according to the legal requirements of the jurisdiction which governs the establishment of the company or other organization. It is not necessary in English law to have witnesses to signatures to a contract which is not a deed. A deed is a special kind of contract, which is required to be used in certain circumstances, such as for the sale of land. Outsourcing contracts do not need to conform to the formalities associated with deeds. However, local authorities and other public organizations may have standing orders which require contracts above a certain value to be executed as deeds. If a contract is to be a deed, it must be clear from its contents that it is intended to be a deed, and it must be executed under the corporate common seal or signed on behalf of a company by any person acting under the company's authority. A document signed by a director and the secretary of a company or by two directors of the company and expressed as being executed by the company has the same effect as if executed under the common seal of the company. Rules for the correct execution of contracts by supplier or customer organizations not governed by English law must be conformed to.

Third parties who are involved in the outsourcing, such as end users of the customer, or sub-contractors of the supplier, must have their own contracts with the customer or supplier respectively, which will mirror the relevant rights and obligations appearing in the outsourcing agreement.

Assignment and novation

Unless there is an express prohibition against assignment in the contract, under English law either party may assign the benefit of the contract to another party. An assignment is the transfer of part or all of the benefits of the contract. The contract remains in effect, but the rights of one party, 'the assignor', such as the supplier's right to payment, may be transferred to another party, 'the assignee'. The assignee may then enforce the payment terms in the contract against the customer. The customer will still be able to enforce the contract against the original supplier, whose obligations of providing services are not transferred through the assignment.

It is normal for the contract to place some restrictions on either party's ability to assign it. A clause prohibiting assignment without the prior consent of the other party to the contract is commonly found. This gives the option of refusal of a proposed new relationship with an unsuitable or undesirable assignee. In practice, a customer may want the right to assign the contract if it is likely that during the term of the contract its corporate structure of associated companies should change, or if the part of the organization for which the services are being supplied is to be sold off. In this case, the customer might require a clause stating that assignment by the customer to its related companies or to a third party will be permitted. In circumstances in which the assignor is a company within a group of companies and the proposed assignee is another company in that group, assignment may be acceptable to the supplier.

If assignment is to be permitted, a safeguard may be introduced by making the assignment subject to the other party's consent. It may be agreed that this consent should not be withheld unreasonably. This will give an opportunity to examine the financial viability of the proposed assignee company and any previous unsatisfactory relationship between the non-assigning company and the proposed assignee.

Sometimes reciprocity is required in the negotiated assignment provisions, or there may be special reasons for permitting or forbidding assignment altogether.

A 'novation' agreement replaces a contract. This will be desirable if the terms and conditions are being significantly varied, or in a situation where the original parties to the contract agree that a third party should take the place of one of them. The effect of a novation agreement is to extinguish the original contract and create a new one. This is often a useful opportunity to review the terms to ensure that they are all still applicable, and to consider whether new terms should be negotiated. As a new contract, the novation agreement should state the rights and obligations of each of the three parties; both the original parties and the party taking over, and all of them should sign it.

Intention to proceed

It occasionally happens that the supplier's sales representatives want to get an early assurance by the customer that its intent to proceed is serious, especially where it is appreciated that negotiations may be protracted. A letter of intent may be requested. Other names for documents with equivalent purposes are 'heads of terms', 'heads of agreement', 'memorandum of understanding'. The language and format of the document are matters of choice. It may be worded as an informal letter or it may be constructed as an intimidating-looking paper. It will set out the intentions of one party or of both, and outline any key terms already known.

It should be a matter for careful decision whether such a document is really necessary. It may be of some benefit where it is desirable to keep the Board of either organization informed, or to avoid misunderstandings, or to clarify the steps to be taken, or to flush out major areas of contention early. It may be of no advantage where it is requested only because of a sales representative's anticipated commission.

The document will need care in drafting, to avoid unlooked for obligations and also because it will set the tone for further negotiations, the scope for which should not be unnecessarily constrained. It may not be intended to be legally binding, and it is normally highly advisable that it should not have the status of legal enforceability when the parties are in the early stages of negotiations. The most usual way of indicating this is by using the words 'subject to contract', to show that it is not intended to commit the parties. This is a well understood formula, although not foolproof. Other similar phrases do not have the same conciseness and wide acceptance – for example terms such as 'subject to Board approval' or 'provisional' or 'awaiting formal contract' may be ambiguous as to whether an enforceable agreement has been made in any respect, and therefore should not be used.

In drafting the letter of intent, only the agreed commercial principles should be set out, not any details. It must be clear that all the statements made will be subject to any third party involvement, such as the consents required for assignment of software licences. It may be appropriate to suggest a contract timetable. It should be openly acknowledged that it is not a complete statement of the parties' objectives.

Separately from the letter of intent itself, other agreements preliminary to the contract may be required. If confidentiality is of concern, a binding non-disclosure agreement should be separately made, as discussed in Chapter 2. There may be circumstances in which the supplier can request a 'lock-out' agreement, meaning that the customer will not negotiate with third parties for a specified period, perhaps in return for the supplier entering into negotiations with third party software suppliers or starting its investigation of the customer's service level requirements.

An 'agreement to agree' is not legally enforceable under English law. There are too many potential escapes.

Planning the contract

A good contract will need careful planning from the early stages of considering outsourcing.

At the stage of inviting tenders, some of the contract criteria will already be known. For example, local authority contracts often have standard provisions about compliance with non-discriminatory legislation. It is advisable for a customer to include a contract outline or a basic contract with its invitation to tender. Suppliers themselves will have basic terms on which it is profitable for them to conduct business, and may wish to include these as part of their tender responses.

There are different views on what terms should be set out by the customer in the contract attached to the invitation to tender. One opinion held by some experienced contract negotiators is that all the terms should be included to which the customer would ideally wish the supplier to be committed. An alternative valid negotiating position is that only those terms which are essential and not negotiable, or which are highly desirable, should be set out in the documentation for the invitation to tender. There is no point in deterring potential bidders by contract requirements which are more idealistic than realistic and which bidders know that they would not be able to accept.

Once the supplier has been selected, the provisions of the contract need to be negotiated and agreed. If the contract is for a large scale outsourcing, the supplier will need to obtain accurate information about all aspects of the services being outsourced, similar to the process of 'due diligence' which is carried out on the sale of a business. In this case its purpose is to investigate, inspect, evaluate and verify the information, condition and legal status of what is being outsourced. The customer will disclose such matters as third party contracts, software licences and support agreements, financial details, insurances, leases, property and other proprietary rights, contractor contracts, employment policies, union affairs, disciplinary issues, terms of employment. A limited part of this information could be supplied at the stage when the invitation to tender is made, so that suppliers have sufficient knowledge to submit 'educated' bids. Much will be too sensitive to disclose at this early point, even in the unlikely event of it being readily available.

Most of this information will need to be included in the contract or incorporated into it, or referred to in it. At the outset of negotiations a substantial amount of detail will not be known and the information will have to be collated. A data room may be set up for this process, a location which can be dedicated to storing relevant information and copies of documents, much of which may be confidential.

The customer may already have defined the service levels, in which case the supplier needs to confirm that they are reasonable and can continue to be achieved, but it is far more usual for them to be drawn up and agreed during the negotiations. The time involved in this must not be underestimated. Occasionally they are not agreed until after the contract formally comes into effect – although this is highly inadvisable from the customer's perspective, and not to be recommended. Many other decisions which need to be taken will emerge during the negotiations, such as how much weekly or monthly management liaison there should be.

Generally speaking, there is likely to be an enormous amount of work to be done in gathering and establishing the information required. This exercise may be carried out by the customer alone or with the supplier's participation.

For these reasons, an outsourcing contract will take some time to finalise. It can take several months to sort out the commercial aspects and technical issues as well as the legal requirements. The earlier the process is initiated, the fewer pressures there will be to take quick decisions just to keep the process moving. Decisions taken impulsively in this way are not likely to be as sound as those made when there has been time to consider all the surrounding circumstances. There are bound to be differences of opinion and approach, but the earlier these can be aired in an atmosphere where everyone is keen to reach the right outcome, the better the result is likely to be. Any problems which arise should be confronted so that they may be resolved. If they are ignored, they will not go away, and the longer they remain, the more difficult it will get to find solutions. Whether from the supplier or the customer's point of view, it makes far more sense to sort out problems and find common ground *before* the contract is signed.

A contract negotiation timetable and plan may be prepared, identifying key target dates and events, with dates set for signing the contract and for the outsourcing services to commence. This can be useful to keep up the momentum. However, deadlines are often imposed arbitrarily or for political reasons. If these are unrealistic in the light of the work that has to be done, the decisions which need to be taken and the consensus that must be reached, they can introduce undesirable stress into the process of negotiation. The customer may wish the start of the outsourcing service to coincide with the start of its financial year or from termination of the lease on the computer premises, or the contract may have to be signed before the Chief Executive goes on holiday. The sales representatives of the outsourcing supplier may have their own compelling reasons for wanting the deal to be struck by the end of a particular quarter.

The resources to use in negotiating

The actress Sandi Toksvig once said that in Equity, the actors' union, at any one time there is about 90 per cent unemployment. So actors' negotiations work along the lines of the director saying to the actors, 'You're going to have to take a pay cut,' and the actors close the deal by saying 'Well, all right, then.'[1] Negotiating strategy for outsourcing should be more positive than this, rather as defined by Mark McCormack, as 'the mediation between competing interests, with an eye towards a mutually profitable, face-saving, and, whenever possible, relationship-preserving result.'[2]

Goodwill and integrity on both sides are as crucial in negotiating the contract as in carrying out the services.

The contract will cover matters which are unfamiliar to the average customer's managers and normal legal advisers. In addition, for public authorities and utilities, access to expertise in European Union procurement law is necessary, as discussed in Chapter 3. For a large scale outsourcing contract, professional specialist contract advice should be seriously considered by the customer as part of its investment in outsourcing. An outsourcing legal expert will be experienced in knowing what must be covered, in reflecting the commercial terms in legal language by careful drafting, and in advising on the negotiations. Different organizations will have different styles of making the best use of the expertise, depending on their own preferences, in deciding whether or not there should be a legal presence at all the negotiations, in whether or not to expect lawyers to review every technical IT document, and so on. Although any in-house legal advisers will typically not be experienced in handling outsourcing contracts, they will advise on general points of the organization's legal policy, and should stay informed on the progress of the contract negotiations.

For a large contract, a small team may be picked to co-ordinate and progress it, including technical, financial, human resources and legal expertise, perhaps with a core negotiating team backed up by background advisers in specialist areas. The individuals involved in the negotiating need clear roles, a target

---

1   Quoted in an article in *Good Housekeeping* magazine, October 1995.
2   *What They Didn't Teach Me At Yale Law School*, Mark McCormack, Fontana Paperbacks 1988.

and a strategy, and the authority to make most of the decisions without having constantly to refer them and delay the process.

The customer needs demonstrable commitment at Board level. One of the directors may be appointed as the senior member of the co-ordinating team. There should be at least a direct reporting relationship from the team leader to a nominated director at Board level or its equivalent in a non-corporate organization. If an internal appointment is to be made to the role of customer liaison manager, that person should be involved at an early stage, since that is where the overall responsibility will lie for monitoring and managing the contract and for implementing change.

A narrow legalistic approach is inadvisable. It does not make for a good working relationship, and in any event it will be impossible to cover every eventuality. However, certain legal obligations do have to be taken into account, such as the duty to consult on behalf of staff, mentioned in Chapter 6. Records of what was negotiated may have to be kept to demonstrate that the correct procurement process was followed, in case of legal challenge by other bidders.

A confrontational approach is not an effective way to proceed. Certainly it is essential for one party to introduce the provisions it needs that the other party will not think of proposing. The selected starting point may also be the ideal position for that party, since negotiation is not going to increase the advantage. However, there is no point in putting forward a preferred option that it is known will be rejected out of hand for good reason. The many hours, days and weeks invested in negotiations, discussions and arguments should be for the purpose of reaching a balanced consensus which is acceptable to both parties. Time should not be wasted in considering unrealistic wishes.

It can be a salutary experience to compare the final contract against early drafts. However, the pressures to conclude negotiations and produce a workable contract usually mean that there is no time, or indeed necessity, to do this. Moreover, the requirements on both sides will be subject to modification and compromise while the negotiations are taking place.

Contract structure

The structure of an outsourcing agreement is likely to comprise more than one single contract document in an arrangement of any complexity, so that a number of linked agreements will normally be customised to the particular set of circumstances. The focus of this book is on the agreement for services, which will cover the scope of the services. Service levels, pricing and payment will logically form part of this agreement, but may be dealt with as separate but intrinsically linked documents. There may be several other related agreements, each a separate contract but mutually interdependent, and expressly stated to be so. A business transfer agreement will be drawn up where the sale, leasing and purchase of premises and other assets are to be included as part of the outsourcing. If land or buildings are being transferred, there will also be property contracts. There will be a separate agreement if staff are transferring from the customer to the supplier. These matters are discussed in Chapters 5 and 6 respectively.

There may be other discrete contracts for individual but associated applications or functions, or for logically independent services; such as for disaster recovery if some unusual event were to prevent the normal provision of the services, or for consultancy arrangements. There may be a systems development agreement where the outsourcing is to a supplier who will be first developing a new system for its customer, and then running it.

Each of these agreements may have its own detailed schedules incorporated. They will all be formally linked so that they all work together and are enforceable together.

One single bound document may be a tidy but optimistic ambition which is not usually achievable in practice or even advisable. If the contract document consists of a thick bundle of papers, as it may be where there are service level agreements or other schedules or appendices, it will be inconvenient and awkward to try to find a particular provision. One means of organising the paperwork is to have the principal contract conditions in the main part of the contract, and to have all the information which may vary during the course of the arrangement set out in appendices or schedules. Any linked agreements such as the service level agreements will logically form part of the overall contract terms and conditions, but can be kept physically as separate documents. This will make it easier to refer to change control procedures, or how to resolve a dispute, or how to conduct the formal liaison meetings, or the charging rates, or what the service levels should be. It is also likely that those staff who need to know what the contract says will need access only to certain information. If they need to refer to service levels or to change control procedures, they will not need to know the charging basis or the limits of liability.

A contract structure and format with separate schedules will help to achieve this during the course of the contract, and build flexibility into the contract as it progresses. Thus updated conditions may be included relatively easily by replacing the schedule concerned, rather than modifying the whole agreement or having updating riders as separate pieces of paper for the clauses altered. Certain documents may be clearly referenced without having to form part of the whole contract documentation, for example a customer may require the supplier to abide by health and safety procedures, which can be identified without having to be an intrinsic part of the contract wording.

The more complex the arrangements, the more that business process re-engineering forms part of the requirements, the more unlikely it will be that every event that might occur will be envisaged and provision made to deal with the consequences. The contract may in some places deliberately contain statements of intent rather than consist at all points of a rigorous record of each party's rights and obligations. The contract may specify methods whereby decisions should be taken during the course of the provision of the services, such as the procedures for evaluating variations required to the services. Legal exactitude must be tempered by flexibility.

Contract formalities

> '... the double challenge in composing any sort of document: keep it simple, but make it complete. The tension between those two goals is not always easy to resolve.'[3]

The formality of the wording is a matter of preference. How far technical terms should be spelt out for the uninitiated, the length of the sentences, the manner in which the legal requirements are stated, are relatively unimportant questions of style. The contract should be intelligible to those who need to understand it, in reasonably sized print and in a format and presentation which is reader friendly rather than daunting. From a practical perspective, it is helpful for the pages to be numbered, and for there to be a contents page, including a list of the schedules. It is useful for its word processing file reference, version and date, to be recorded at some point. It should be bound in such a way that it will not readily disintegrate. All this may seem to be stating the obvious, but does not always happen in practice, especially where pressures of time have affected the negotiation.

---

3   *What They Didn't Teach Me At Yale Law School*, Mark McCormack, Fontana Paperbacks 1988.

A contract will conventionally commence by setting out the names and addresses of the parties, followed by the 'Recitals', which are summarised statements of the purposes of the contract and perhaps the events leading up to the formation of the contract. Many contracts continue with long preambles which are not strictly necessary, for example recording that the masculine includes the feminine or that the singular includes the plural. This is automatically the case under English law.[4]

For a contract comprising a number of related agreements, it should be clear which agreement and schedule takes precedence in which sequence in the event of any conflicting terms – the longer the agreements and the more of them there are, and in particular if any standard terms and conditions form part of the network of contracts, the more possible it is for there to be occasional contradictory provisions.

Definitions included in the contract should be for those words or terms whose meanings need to be clear and are specific to the contract, and which are used more than once in the body of the contract. Such terms, identified in use by capital initials, will then draw the reader's attention to the fact that they are being used in a particular sense and in a consistent way. The same definitions should apply as far as possible across all the contractual documents and schedules. For example: '"Approved Sub-contractors" means those contractors to the Supplier in relation to the Services approved by the Customer in accordance with the provisions of this Agreement; "Authorised User" means any person who, with the permission of the Customer, has access to the Customer Systems or is a beneficiary of the Services' (such terms with capital initials being themselves defined).

Within the contract, there will be numbered clauses or paragraphs, each referring to one aspect of the contract, and each clause may be divided into sub-clauses. For example, one clause may be headed 'Termination' and its sub-clauses would consist of the different grounds for termination. Schedules may also contain numbered paragraphs. Schedules themselves are often numbered. However, as it may not be clear at the outset of drafting what subject matter will be appropriate to include in schedules, it is easier to draft the contract if the schedules are given titles and referred to as such. Thus, 'Key Personnel Schedule' is more readily identifiable than 'Schedule 5'. Cross-references to clauses or to schedules should always be carefully checked before the contract is finalized, to ensure that all the variations leave the numbering correct.

---

4   Law of Property Act 1925, Section 61.

There need be only one contract document signed by both parties. But if both parties want to hold an original document, there can be two identical contract counterparts, each signed by both parties.

The legal system applicable to the contract, and the procedure for giving notices, are basic provisions included in the contract.

Governing law and jurisdiction

With the increasing popularity of offshoring and global sourcing, discussed in Chapter 14, it is self-evident that the offices of the supplier and of the customer do not always need to be in close proximity, or in the same country. Outsourcing services of various kinds are often carried out in a far remote location.

The contract should be drawn up according to one legal system, and a clause included to state which legal system governs the interpretation of the wording and the operation of the provisions, and which courts are to have jurisdiction if a dispute leads to legal proceedings. (Dispute resolution is discussed in Chapter 13.) Normally if either party is a company or another type of organization with an address in England or Wales, a contract statement will be made to the effect that the contract will be governed and interpreted by the law of England and Wales. The discussions in this book proceed on the basis of this legal jurisdiction.

Notices

One clause will specify what is required for formal notification of matters relating to the contract, for example notice to implement a benchmarking exercise or notice to terminate the contract.

The notice must be precise and in writing. The clause will specify to whom and at which address the notice should be sent, such as the Company Secretary or the Solicitor's Department, who will be responsible for acting on it. Job titles are preferable in being more permanent than named individuals. It will state how the notice may be delivered, and when it is to be received.

A standard provision requires notices to be delivered personally or sent by the postal system, with a deemed delivery date which will depend on the respective locations of the parties, allowing for a reasonable time, and the rules of different postal systems if the parties do not belong to the same jurisdiction, and the laws on notice differ. For example, recorded delivery is useful for evidential purposes within the UK, and there are often equivalent arrangements abroad.

The contract and nothing but the contract

A 'representation' is a legal term used for a statement made by one of the parties before the contract has been agreed. The contract will normally include a provision that neither party has relied on any representations except any which are recorded within the contract, and that nothing written or verbal will be of any effect unless set out in the printed contract, or incorporated by inclusion or reference in a schedule or appendix. Specifically, liability will be excluded for non-fraudulent pre-contract representations. The purpose of this provision is to ensure that the parties have agreed on the matters relevant in their decision to enter into the contract.

Each party should scrutinise correspondence, documents, sales brochures, notes of meetings held, from the time they first began to negotiate, for any statements made which were important in the decision to go ahead with the other party. For example, a letter by the sales director of the outsourcing company setting out the company's experience with similar sized companies in the same market area as the customer, might have been important to the customer in selecting that supplier as having the relevant experience. A statement made by the customer that it would be increasing its strategic IT expenditure long term in the area being outsourced may be significant for the supplier in deciding on making a response to tender.

Ideally any representation being relied on by either party should be set out in the formal agreement as a term of the contract. Alternatively a representation may be incorporated by reference to the date of the letter or meeting when the representation was made, if this can be done without introducing ambiguity, or the correspondence or note of the meeting concerned can be attached as a schedule to the main agreement.

The exclusion of liability for pre-contract representations is legally permitted only subject to a test of 'reasonableness'.[5] The actual wording and surrounding circumstances would be reviewed carefully in the event of a dispute if the clause were ever to be challenged in the courts. If the contract is a negotiated agreement so that the clause has been positively agreed, and if

---

5   Misrepresentation Act 1967.

there is correspondence or there are any notes of meetings or other statements about events which took place before the execution of the contract which are recorded in the contract, it is likely that the clause will be regarded at law as reasonable (subject to an exception if the representation was fraudulent).

A contract can be rescinded or set aside as a result of a misrepresentation which the other party relied on in entering into the contract, even if the misrepresentation had been made negligently or even innocently – for example, by a sales representative who honestly believed what he was saying at the time.

If the other party has no reasonable grounds for having made the representation, damages can be claimed by the party not at fault as the amount necessary for that party to be reinstated to the same situation as if the contract had not been made. This is different from the position that the party would have been in had the representation been true. Damages for misrepresentation do not compensate for any loss of bargain or loss of profit. However, if the innocent party can show that it suffered loss as a result of relying on a misrepresentation made fraudulently, then damages may be recovered for that loss.[6] One example of fraudulent representation arose where the customer had agreed to the contract on the basis that a back-to-back contract would be made by the supplier with a sub-contractor. However, the supplier knew that the sub-contractor had refused to enter into the back-to-back contract, because it believed that the resources had been underestimated.[7] It therefore makes sense to include any important commitment made by either party as a warranty term in the contract. The remedy for any breach of warranty is the amount necessary to restore the injured party to the position it would have been in if the warranty had been true.

In a contract lasting for any length of time, there will be adjustments and variations made while the contract is in force. To cater for these, the contract should have a clause permitting variations to the wording to be made under specific circumstances: that they are in writing, dated after the contract date – otherwise they would conflict with the requirement for everything to be contained in the contract at the time of signature – and signed by both parties to show that the modification has been agreed. There may reasonably be a requirement that the status of the signatories to contract variations should be at the same level as that of the original signatories.

---

6   Misrepresentation Act 1967.
7   *South West Water Services Ltd v International Computers Ltd* [1999] BLR 420, QBD (T&CC).

Contract philosophy

A successfully negotiated outsourcing contract should not be hidden away (or worse still, lost) once it has been signed. It should remain available to the people operating and monitoring the outsourcing services, as a source for referring to procedures, parameters and service levels. Not everyone will need to know all the intricacies and complexities, but different features will be relevant to different managers of the contract process.

If the contract is long and complicated with a number of schedules, a user guide to cover the points which will arise day by day will be a very useful document. It does not need to cover every aspect of the contract, and it should not be in language which is remotely legalistic, but should be a practical guide to the way the agreement works.

However much trust the parties believe they have in working together, this should never be an excuse for the contract requirements not to be properly defined. The business circumstances of either party may alter. Any of the people running the outsourcing day-to-day, the members of the management board or other relevant personnel of either the supplier or the customer, may move away to different work or to another company. Their successors may lack the original commitment or the knowledge of what had been discussed during the negotiations.

The contract should allow for the different objectives of the supplier and the customer. For the supplier, the contract is a source of income. For the customer the contract is for the provision of services affecting its business.

The balance of control in monitoring the contract should lie with the customer. This is not to say that in all circumstances control will be given to existing managers of the customer organization who were formerly responsible for the IT operation. Although it will often be the case that the customer's IT manager becomes the services manager under the new regime, it may be necessary for the customer to make a new appointment of a services manager or a liaison manager, or to take a decision to bring in external consultants for management of the process. Yet the day-to-day outsourcing operation should continue to be monitored and controlled from a strategic point of view by representatives of the customer. For this to be effective, there should be a reporting channel for the customer manager, whether this is an internal or an external service function in the organization, direct to the Board or its equivalent level. This is discussed further in Chapter 9.

In negotiating the contract, there should be mutual respect for the parties' perspectives. The supplier must be able to make a profit. The customer must be facilitated in running its business. It is always helpful to give reasons why a particular requirement is needed. This enables consensus to be reached, if necessary by examining other ways of achieving the objective.

If the negotiating process is unsatisfactory and confrontational, each party should review whether the relationship is going to work.

A one-sided contract for outsourcing will benefit neither the supplier nor the customer in the long term. Arm's length co-operation is essential to the success of outsourcing.

Selecting a Supplier

Selecting a supplier

The right choice of supplier is crucial. The selection process will take time, preceding the detailed drafting and negotiation of the contract. The customer should allow for adequate resources and management time at the early stages of planning for the outsourcing bid. (The public sector has specific rules for this, as discussed in Chapter 3.)

The invitation to prospective suppliers will almost always be made before the decision to outsource becomes public knowledge. Assurances that the customer's confidentiality will be respected must first be obtained.

The invitation to tender must be carefully prepared to ensure that the information made available to the tenderers will be sufficient and at the appropriate level of detail to enable them to put forward meaningful bids to demonstrate their competence and suitability and for them to price the contract.

The consequences of making the wrong choice of supplier will be highly undesirable, even if a carefully drawn contract can minimise the effects. In the selection process, the various elements of quality, cost, expertise, compatibility and the essential characteristics of the supplier must be carefully assessed.

As well as the customer, the potential suppliers will be investing time, effort and resources in bidding for the work. By a process of elimination, a number of apparently suitable suppliers will be reduced to one. This process should be seen to be conducted by the customer fairly and objectively. The suppliers should be carrying out their own evaluation of whether the potential business is within their competence and will enable profit opportunities with proper management of the risks identified. They need to confirm that the tender information is accurate.

While 'partnership' and 'partnering' are terms often quoted, by suppliers rather more frequently than by customers, the outsourcing contract will normally be entered into between the supplier and the customer as independent parties.

Customer preparation

Early predictors of eventual outsourcing success are that the customer should have clear objectives, and that there should be project sponsorship at a senior level.

One of the first considerations by the customer should be whether outsourcing is in fact the most effective means of providing the most appropriate services. Would it be practicable to reach the same objective by bringing in experienced project managers, or numbers of technically skilled resources on a consultancy or services basis as and when required without any long term commitment?

Different kinds of outsourcing requirements will appeal to different suppliers according to their expertise. An unambiguous statement of business objectives will help attract the appropriate suppliers. Where the outsourced services proposed by the customer are limited, low in value, and for routine applications, the supplier's perception, probably well founded, will be that there would be minimal potential for further work in the future. Alternatively, a customer may be looking for its current IT function to be wholly outsourced prior to the acquisition of new systems and new services, which will be developed and provided by the supplier. If the customer will also be demanding business process re-engineering for IT reorganization, this will attract outsourcing suppliers who are more interested in adding value to their services through developing innovative ideas for efficiencies and expansion of the customer's IT needs.

Informed discussions within the customer organization should lead to an understanding of what is to be specified in the invitation to tender and what is to be excluded.

It may be appropriate to consider taking the invitation to tender as a two-stage process, the first being the pre-qualification stage to invite expressions of interest. From these responses, which may vary in the broad solutions proposed, the customer may decide on the particular approach, and narrow down the invitation in the second stage to those suppliers who can develop a detailed response according to that approach.

The exploratory stage of learning about the possibilities of the various approaches may therefore be successfully addressed as a separate pre-procurement exercise. Suppliers may be engaged in debate on that basis, which can provide a legitimate opportunity for them to promote what they can do, while various options are still open. This will both assist the customer in its decision making on the form of outsourcing – and may incidentally help to identify suitable suppliers who will be invited to make proposals. Following this decision on the form and scope of the outsourcing, a statement of requirements or invitation to tender may be issued and specific responses sought.

This is the time to consider whether the work can be split up. It may not be necessary for the customer to appoint one single outsourcing supplier. It is generally less risky to outsource functions selectively to more than one supplier. The customer must ensure that there is ownership of, and therefore ultimate responsibility for, the outsourcing contract negotiations, through the project sponsorship role. For outsourcing which is related in any way to a company's business strategy and objectives (in contrast to, for example, outsourcing a self-contained legacy system which will be superseded in a few years), the sponsorship function should be at Board level.

To see the selection process through, a project manager should be appointed, who may be separate from the project sponsor. For outsourcing on a large scale, a team of representatives may assist the project manager, drawn in from all the line functions affected. This may include human resources, estate management, financial management, procurement, and possibly a spokesperson for the business end users, to harness their enthusiasm early, and to keep them informed.

As a matter of policy, the director of the IT function in the organization ought normally to be closely involved, perhaps as project sponsor if at Board level, or as project manager with responsibility for the management of the outsourcing selection and contract negotiation. There must in any event be sufficient professional competence to assess the technical validity and quality of proposals or tenders.

Prospective suppliers should be identified and asked if they would be interested in tendering. The customer's in-house team may be asked to put in a bid as well. If there is an in-house bid, it is even more important how the bidding process is managed.

Whatever the reasons for considering outsourcing, if the in-house IT team is being given the opportunity to put forward a proposal, their bid must be treated equally seriously to the external bids. On the other hand, if the exercise is to be undertaken, it must not be a waste of time for the external applicant bidders. There should be an open competitive tender.

If the in-house bid is unsuccessful, the team in place will be suffering a loss of morale, and yet will still be expected to continue working up until the time the contract is signed and the supplier takes over. The genuine risk here is of losing skill and experience through resignations which could leave the customer exposed. Thus the shorter the time between the selection of the supplier and commencement of the outsourcing, the better, subject to there being suffficient time to negotiate a sound contract. In certain circumstances the outsourcing supplier appointed may be able to provide interim resources on a consultancy basis, until the outsourcing contract is finalized.

Consultants

The customer's outsourcing team should consider appointing consultants with wide outsourcing expertise at the outset, to give up to date advice from their experience. If the customer organization lacks the competence to manage the selection process or if there are political reasons for not making an internal appointment, the consultants may assume an important and influential role.

Among the characteristics essential for consultants are suitable experience, demonstrable integrity, and an established methodology for giving their advice. Client references should be followed up. The consultants should be genuinely independent, in order to be able to advise objectively on setting strategy and in managing the bid process, and there is therefore a very strong case for arguing that they should be free from any links with outsourcing companies. In any event, it is generally highly undesirable, although not unknown, for a consultants' firm to advise a customer in making the decision as to outsourcing, thereby acquiring in-depth knowledge of the customer's business, and then to succeed in getting the work either without any competition or by virtue of the advantages they will have gained over any other suppliers who enter the bid process later.

Confidentiality

The customer must take confidentiality seriously from the start – before employing the services of outsourcing consultants or issuing the invitation to tender. It is advisable at the early stages to confine the knowledge that outsourcing is an option under consideration to a very few people, both within the customer's organization and externally. Moreover, in issuing the invitation to tender or in subsequent investigation by suppliers in order to produce their responses, the customer may have to make business information available which is not for general circulation.

The customer should therefore insist on a non-disclosure agreement being signed by any outsourcing consultants whose services are being used, and if appropriate, by any prospective suppliers. To be effective, this must be done in advance of any confidential information being made known to them.

A simple non-disclosure agreement for suppliers would state that in consideration of the disclosure of all information in the invitation to tender about the proprietary, legal, business and technical matters of the customer, and other related information, the recipient of the information should use it only for the business purpose of making its response. The information should not be further disclosed, nor copied except as necessary, and should be furnished only to those of the supplier's employees who need to know it.

For the supplier's benefit, there will be certain exceptions to what is regarded as confidential. These will include the disclosure of necessary information by the supplier to its accountants, legal advisers or any officials where there are legislative requirements. Information already known or within the public domain will also be excepted from confidentiality as will general concepts of information technology which would not be protectable. At the same time the agreement can make it clear that the customer is not representing that there will inevitably be any further contracts in respect of the information; and that either party is at liberty to enter into similar agreements with other parties. The more coherently the requirements are set out, the easier the agreement will be to understand and enforce.

The supplier should agree not to disclose its customer's name in promotional materials or otherwise without consent. This provision may be overridden by the terms of the outsourcing contract once it becomes public knowledge, or it may be reinforced by the later agreement if it is a sensitive issue for the customer for any reason.

The invitation to tender and any other documents supplied should clearly be marked as confidential, for limited circulation and not to be copied, as appropriate. A footer on each page may carry the message that the information has been supplied in confidence and is subject to the non-disclosure agreement having been signed. Copyright notices are helpful although not necessary.

The customer may use a front page disclaimer to emphasize that it is not committed to proceeding with outsourcing. This may state that the information is provided on the basis that the document is an 'invitation to treat' and not a contractual offer; that any costs incurred by the supplier in preparing the response will be their own; that although all efforts have been made to ensure that the information is correct, it is not warranted to be accurate or comprehensive; and that no undertaking is given that a supplier will be appointed resulting from any responses to the invitation to tender or otherwise.

In conjunction with this, the customer should exercise care in what it does disclose, as a matter of sensible practice. The potential suppliers must have access to all information necessary for them to be able to make a reasonable bid. However, they should be able to see that the customer itself regards the need for confidentiality seriously. It is far easier to be pre-emptive than to have to react by invoking the agreement once any damage has been done.

Conversely, in their responses to the tender, potential suppliers will be disclosing commercially sensitive information about their charges, proposed methodologies and solutions and information about their own businesses. Customers must avoid divulging elements of one potential supplier's bid to any others. If one supplier asks for information, it needs to be clear whether the answer to that question will be conveyed to all suppliers so that they all have identical information. The disadvantage is that this could prevent a potential bidder from asking for information to support an innovative bid, as other suppliers might gain some insight into their planning. Thus suppliers' responses should be marked as confidential and not for copying, for disclosure within the customer organization only to those individuals who need to know and to the customer's advisers.

The invitation to tender

In drawing up the invitation to tender, the customer should be conscious of the fact that the bid process can be extremely expensive for bidders, only one of whom is going to succeed. An express statement that the supplier's costs of tendering will not be met may be appropriate.

Sufficient information must be provided to enable the potential suppliers to weigh up their experience in the light of the stated requirements and their ability to carry out the work profitably, so that they may realistically assess whether it is a contract that they will want.

It is worth the customer considering the number of suppliers it expects to be shortlisted. A large number is not ideal, and will mean that several suppliers will be investing time unnecessarily in responding.

The invitation to tender should address the objectives of outsourcing in context, defining the scope by identifying the services required. It will include, in detail:

- the organizational structure and description of the organization;

- the objectives for the outsourcing, and whether there has been previous or existing outsourcing for the same area;

- whether there are other outsourcing providers working with the customer, or whether there will be scope for future outsourcing requirements separately from this one, for the same or for a different provider;

- current services and service levels;

- current problems;

- exclusions from the scope of outsourcing;

- details of assets, premises and staff, and whether or not the intention is to include these within the outsourcing.

Suppliers should be asked to demonstrate generally:

- their understanding of the requirements;

- how they intend to provide the services;

- their proposed fees and charges;

- their proposed management of the relationship.

For some areas much detail will be available and any related performance criteria already known. Others will be sketchy. The focus should be on outputs, not methods, except where it is essential for certain organizational procedures to be followed. Links with other existing systems or services which are not part of the invitations to tender should be identified, and any standards with which the supplier will be expected to conform.

It is useful for a management synopsis and a list of contents to be provided at the beginning of the response.

Some ground rules may be laid down. The invitation to tender will delineate the criteria for selecting and evaluating the tenders. It should state that all contacts in connection with the tender should be made only through designated parties, named and whose names and locations, telephone and email addresses, are given. This will be partly for confidentiality reasons, if the fact of going out to tender is not widely known within the customer organization. Potential suppliers may also expect to have to spend time with the customer to find out more about its IT department's operation and resources in order to make their bids. If one person has responsibility in the customer's organization, contacts can be properly organized through one channel, giving all the suppliers equal opportunities, and avoiding conflicts, early disclosure or unnecessary work interruptions. A further reason is to ensure that the project manager keeps effective control of the bid process, to prevent bidders from thinking that they can achieve results by side-stepping the agreed processes, for example by making overtures directly to senior directors.

The customer may categorically reserve the right to disqualify bidders who do not respond in the format requested. In any event, it will be far easier to compare responses which follow the same sequence. References should be requested and followed up. In addition, the customer may want to make it clear that it retains control: that it reserves the right to amend the document, and that it is not obliged to proceed by awarding a tender. It may state that the selection will be based on various criteria, and not cost alone.

The customer may give an indicative timetable without having to make a commitment to a specific schedule. It would be reasonable to state the time frame within which presentations will be given from those bids short listed, and an anticipated date by which the selection of supplier will be made. Actual dates should be specified only if they are likely to be adhered to.

Tenderers will be given a deadline for responding to the invitation to tender, which should allow enough time for a thorough response to be given. Their response to the invitation to tender will be a document setting out the ways in which they believe they can meet the requirements, and they may also be given the opportunity of making a presentation.

Criteria in choosing the supplier

In selecting a supplier, its financial viability and reliability are important elements. It is an essential prerequisite to an ongoing working relationship that supplier and customer should both feel comfortable about building a long term co-operative relationship together. The following are basic questions for including in the invitation to tender, which the customer should expand as appropriate and which will need positive answers from the supplier. Of course costs will be a major consideration, but not irrespective of other factors.

EXPERIENCE

- What is the supplier's company history and track record? How many years experience does the supplier have in outsourcing? Is it a new company or has this work developed logically from what it was doing before? Are outsourcing services part of the supplier's core business, or is more time spent in publishing or implementing software?

- How many staff are there? Is there a structure to allow for career development, with different levels of experience and reporting relationships? Is there evidence of investment by the supplier in the resources needed to support the service?

- For how many clients are outsourcing services being provided? Are references willingly given? Are any clients similar to the potential customer in type of business, size, installation? Are any existing clients direct competitors of the customer? Would this cause a problem?

- Does the supplier have extensive experience of the customer's operating platforms, configurations and systems?

- What is the size of the outsourcing company? Only a handful would be able to claim that they would be capable of handling certain public sector tenders or other large-scale outsourcings alone.

QUALITY

- What evidence is there of the skill, professional qualifications and experience of the supplier's staff?

- What is the supplier's attitude to quality measurement and management?

- Is there any certification such as *Investors in People* or ISO 9000, and what would this mean in practice for the customer?

COMPATIBILITY

- Will the supplier and customer have shared expectations in terms of cultural match, treatment of staff, codes of practice, shared vision of technology, style of management?

- Is the business language similar? Are management attitudes consistent? This will be particularly significant if the customer's staff are to be transferred.

STAFF

- What will the career prospects, training opportunities, pension arrangements and benefits be for transferred staff?

FLEXIBILITY

- Is the supplier independent of hardware manufacturers and software suppliers?

- Will the supplier be able to support future business requirements in terms of expansion and change to the computer systems?

- Is the supplier innovative? Will different strategies for better utilization of resources and assets be proposed?

COSTS

- How do the supplier's costs compare with other suppliers? It is crucial that comparisons between the potential suppliers are made on the same basis; that the costs are for similar services and cover equivalent matters, ascertaining that like is being compared with like.

FINANCIAL VIABILITY

- Is the outsourcing supplier a subsidiary company within a larger group? Who is the real owner of the company? If a risk is perceived in awarding a contract to a supplier who is a subsidiary, a guarantee or indemnity may be required from the parent company, so that, if the subsidiary's business were to founder, the parent company would take over entire responsibility for the contract. Nevertheless, this should not be a substitute for properly evaluating the financial strength and capability of the supplier.

These requirements, tailored to the customer's needs, should be translated into representations which are confirmed as contractual acknowledgements by the supplier.

The draft contract

A draft contract or contract structure may be included with the invitation to tender. These contractual terms need not be too detailed, but they should be reasonable, as setting the basis for the bid. It should be clarified whether these are non-negotiable. Tenderers should be asked to bid on these contract terms and to include in their tenders any proposed amendments to them, if this is permssible.

The supplier's pricing will be based on its usual terms of business. Its costings for the response can allow for any differences in the terms as required by the customer.

Any modifications or proposals to the contract terms put forward by the tenderers should be evaluated in terms of their legal and commercial effects, and compared with the tenor of the rest of the response. For instance, a supplier may claim to be flexible in providing services to meet varying requirements of the customer and yet object to a contract term permitting changes to the services. If at least the principles of the contract terms can be agreed at this stage, and any differences highlighted, this will make the selection and subsequently the negotiation process fairer and less problematic.

Assessing the suppliers' responses

Evaluation by the customer of the responses should be a rigorous process, to make reasoned comparisons among the tenderers. A list of selection criteria should be drawn up, to ensure a consistent approach by each of the panel members concerned in making the evaluation. If one of the bids is from the in-house team, the technical part of the evaluation should be conducted by an independent professional, such as an external consultant.

A structured, disciplined, transparent and objective evaluation process should be adopted for all but relatively minor selections. This must include predetermined criteria, devised from the customer's statement of requirements, graded according to relative importance both as to the overall topics and individual elements within each topic. Model responses may be constructed for each element on a scale of (for example) adequate to excellent, prepared independently of the contents of any proposal; by this means, proposals can be judged objectively against a common model, rather than being compared with each other. The scoring should make provision for awarding marks on the quality of individual responses, and also for the separate application of a confidence rating for significant elements. The latter may require a verification process, especially where innovative features appear in proposals. The customer will take account of the supplier's response to tender. The suppliers on the final short list may be invited to give a presentation in support of their bids. Preparing for and attending presentations is a time consuming exercise both for suppliers and for customers, and only those few tenderers who are the final serious contenders should be asked to do so.

Supplier presentations should have a clearly defined purpose, such as elucidation of proposals and verification, to be carried out at working level with the evaluation team (or its leaders). The presentations will thus be an opportunity to assess some of the statements made in the individual responses, to follow through those which need expanding, to weigh up the suitability of the approach of the potential suppliers in the context of the customer's culture, and to open up the discussion. The objective is to find the supplier best suited to working with the customer on a long term basis. Information on what is going to be required at the presentations may be provided to the tenderers in advance.

The customer may ask for the presentation to be made by the members of the management team who it is proposed will be delivering the services, in order to meet them. Numbers should be limited. There is no advantage in the supplier bringing along everyone who will be having anything at all to do with the contract. There is, however, benefit in having those members of the team who will be involved if the supplier is successful. Any points in the presentations which were particularly impressive in contributing to the supplier's success should be recorded and agreed, and included in the contract as representations which the customer relied on. The response to tender itself may eventually be incorporated in the contract.

The customer should seek references from the supplier's existing customers, and perhaps site visits for finding out confidence ratings for specific elements.

Other information to be investigated should include the annual report, industry reports, and press articles, together with any reports of litigation.

Confidence in the fairness of the selection procedure is important. Customers should remember that suppliers make large investments of resources, effort and costs in bidding.

Records should be kept of the assessment of the responses to tender and the presentations. A debriefing for those bidders who failed is an essential exercise in the public sector to justify the choice that was made. It is also good practice for the private sector, in assisting the unsuccessful suppliers to understand why the chosen supplier was selected.

Relationship of the parties

The outsourcing relationship must be at arm's length. Circumstances change. Nothing can be relied on to last in a commercial, industrial or public service environment. The parties negotiating the agreement will not necessarily be the same as the parties liaising over the life of the contract to carry out the services.

Suppliers use various terms in discussions and in their promotional literature to denote their ideal relationship with the customer: joint venture, joint sourcing, co-sourcing, partnering, partnership. Although the term 'partnership' is frequently encountered as representing co-operation, communication and commitment, its legal meaning carries specific connotations, being a relationship between two or more parties carrying on a business together with a view to making a profit. The profits – or conversely, the losses – are shared between the parties according to what they agree or in proportion to their capital contribution. Thus business partners are also responsible for each other's debts and other obligations. Partners are agents of the partnership. Any one partner has the power to bind the other partners in relation to obligations incurred to third parties in partnership matters. This is not what an outsourcing relationship is normally about.

Moreover, a true partnership is one kind of 'fiduciary relationship', which implies more onerous responsibilities to partners than those which apply in a normal contractual relationship. It arises where there is a special relationship between the parties concerned, often where one party is in a stronger position than the other, such as employee and employer, or guardian and ward. It is a relationship of trust or confidentiality, legally implying obligations of 'good faith' – honesty, openness and good intentions.

The outsourcing relationship is not therefore a genuine legal partnership, and it is not a term which should be recklessly bandied about in the promotional materials and marketing presentations by suppliers, or used in the contract. The profits of each party derive from different activities. The supplier's profits are the result of providing outsourcing services, and perhaps other sorts of information systems services, to numbers of organizations. If the customer is a profit-making business, its profits will arise from its core business, whether it is in the business of selling goods or of supplying services. The customer may be a different kind of organization, such as a public sector authority providing services of one kind or another, but not for profit. The customer has the ultimate right to terminate the contract if the services are unsatisfactory, or not to renew it.

IT 'partnerships' in commercial projects will be at most a form of joint venture, consortium or partnering agreement, rather than a legally defined partnership.

A commercial joint venture is a relationship in which a business is formed for a deliberate purpose between two or more parties who each take a share. For example, this is one solution for the customer's problem of over-capacity on its mainframe. An outsourcing company may be set up resulting from a management buyout by a customer's former IT managers, or as a joint venture between an outsourcing supplier and the IT department of an organization, first in order to supply IT services to that organization, but with the ultimate aim of extending its supply of services to other organizations. A customer may contribute market and application knowledge for future commercial activities. A supplier's contribution will be in terms of technical skills and commercial awareness. The supplier will be in a position to make more extensive use of the computer facilities or to sell the additional capacity, and for the customer and supplier each to benefit.

Both parties to a joint venture need to be committed to its success, and neither party can easily withdraw from the relationship at an early stage without suffering financially or commercially. There will be additional administrative, legal, audit and management responsibilities to take into account, and without a proper development strategy, the effort involved may not be justifiable.

If the reasons for considering a joint venture vehicle are to develop particular vertical services but the customer has no real interest in long term involvement in its management, the customer could make a financial investment in the supplier in the manner of a venture capitalist in return for a participating preferential dividend for some years with a guaranteed buy-out (at a multiple of profits) at some future point.

If the customer is considering a joint venture in order to benefit from a share of profits obtained from exploiting its transferred assets, a profit-sharing obligation in the outsourcing agreement may be just as effective.

However, these variants are relatively exceptional. The normal outsourcing contract should state unequivocally that the parties are independent of each other. If the supplier is being granted any authority to negotiate licences and hardware contracts or any other terms and conditions on the customer's behalf, this should be stated, and it should be made clear whether the supplier does so in its own name or the customer's, so that this authority is not extended to any other contracts for which it is not intended by the customer.

'Partnering' is a current expression for some contracts, originating in the construction industry. Its elements consist of collaborative working for common objectives (for example, in relation to a third party) and long term commitments. This implies team work in performing the contract and a commitment to making it work, yet without the wholesale commitment of partnership. A partnering contract may reduce confrontation, but it does carry a risk that the relationship will be too close, removing any scope for competition or innovation. However, in an outsourcing relationship it is not the case that the supplier and customer do have common objectives.

The supplier may incidentally be in a position of considerable power in awarding contracts to third parties as part of the outsourcing. The customer may wish to spell out in the contract the boundaries of propriety for its own interests: that the supplier should take no commission, bribe or other financial incentive where it is negotiating third party contracts on behalf of its customer, whether hardware, software or services, and should ensure that all its staff are fully aware of this. One stage less exacting than this which may be acceptable to the customer is that if the supplier is permitted to take commission, it should disclose it openly in advance.

The right choice of supplier for the particular outsourcing requirements is paramount to the success of the relationship.

Public Procurement

CHAPTER

3

The UK has a highly developed outsourced public services industry second only to the US in size. According to a Review of the Public Services Industry report published in 2008,[1] it has grown 130 per cent since 1995, having a turnover of £79 billion. This represents over 13 per cent of all government expenditure, and is estimated to grow to almost £100 billion by 2012.[2] In the UK, as in the rest of the EU, the Civil Service, local authorities and other public sector organizations are regulated at law in their procurement practice. The rules and procedures concerned with the procurement of services, including outsourcing services, in the UK public sector, are known as the 'public procurement regime'.

The public procurement rules apply to contracts in the public sector throughout the 27 EU member states, and also to those states which are now part of the European Free Trade Association ('EFTA') – Norway, Iceland and Liechtenstein. They have also been extended to those countries which are signatories to an international agreement negotiated by the World Trade Organization (WTO), the Government Procurement Agreement. Suppliers from these countries have the same rights and must conform to the same rules as EU suppliers for central government and local authorities. The countries who are signatories to the GPA (in addition to the European Communities) are: Aruba, Canada, Hong Kong China. Israel, Japan, Republic of Korea, Liechtenstein, Norway, Singapore, Switzerland, and the US.

Contracting authorities, as the customers in this context are referred to, must award contracts according to objective criteria, following the procedures.

The full regime applies to public works, public supplies and public services. However, this chapter outlines the basic elements of the public procurement regime applying to services and thus to IT outsourcing services. It can provide only an introduction. Customers affected by the regime are bound to be

---

[1]   http://www.berr.gov.uk/about/economics-statistics/economics-direct+orate/page46965.html.
[2]   *Public Sector Outsourcing: The Big Picture to 2012*, Kable Limited 2007.

familiar with the detailed legal requirements. The legislation is complicated, and specialist legal advice is strongly recommended for suppliers interested in participating, who will need to be familiar with the details.

The legal framework

The legislation which forms the basis of the public procurement regime is the EU's Consolidated Procurement Directive.[3] EU Directives are laws which must be implemented into national legal systems of the member states. In England and Wales, this has been achieved by the Public Contracts Regulations 2006.[4] Separate but equivalent legislation applies in Scotland.[5]

Useful introductory guidance is published online by the Office for Government Contracts.[6]

Utilities, that is to say companies in the water, energy, transport, postal services and telecommunications sectors, are also regulated according to similar although not identical procedures forming part of the procurement regime. This chapter will not consider utilities further.

The importance of public procurement

One general principle fundamental to the EU in promoting social and economic progress is that it should comprise a single internal market for trading in goods and services. This implies that any business within the EU, in whatever country it is based, should be able to bid for work anywhere else in the EU. This principle now applies to all the countries which have entered into the agreements discussed earlier.

When looking at whether this precept works successfully in practice, the public sector is of particular concern because throughout the EU it comprises an enormous market for supply and service contracts.

---

3   Consolidated Procurement Directive 2004/18/EC.
4   These regulations may be found at opsi.gov.uk/si/si2006/uksi_20060005_en.pdf.
5   The Scottish Regulations may be found at the following site, together with guidance from the Scottish Executive: http://www.ogc.gov.uk/procurement_policy_and_application_of_eu_rules_devolved_administrations_.asp.
6   http://www.ogc.gov.uk/procurement_policy_and_application_of_eu_rules_guidance_on_the_2006_regulations_.asp http://www.ogc.gov.uk/documents/Introduction_to_the_EU_rules.pdf.

Nevertheless, national products and services have always tended to be favoured when public money is being spent. Throughout the EU, few contracts in the public sector are awarded outside a national territory. These national markets in the public sector are a major hurdle in preventing the achievement of a genuine internal market in the member states. The belief is that the effects of competition in the commercial market place will ultimately bring savings to tax payers.

The purpose of the public procurement regime

The objective of the public procurement regime is to ensure that all public contracts over a given value are publicized and awarded according to principles of transparency, non-discrimination and competition. This means that the specification of the features demanded must list genuine requirements, there must be open competition and there should be no unfair discrimination in the selection of suppliers. At the same time there are procedures available which offer certain limited remedies at law to suppliers who believe that they have been maltreated, and which provide for legal sanctions against customers where there has been a failure to comply with the rules.

By means of the procurement procedures, public sector bodies can identify a range of contractors in their search for the best value, whether the contractors are based in the UK or in other participating countries.

The benefits for suppliers lie in the potential for securing new and increased business opportunities which they would not otherwise necessarily have known about, not only in the UK but across the member states, by open competition on equal terms within the public sector. At the same time, however, they need to reinforce their position in their home market, where they may themselves be subject to greater competition.

Who has to follow the rules?

'Contracting authorities', having contracts to award for the provision of services, include central and local government and other bodies governed by public law, including various quasi-public entities such as urban development corporations, fire authorities, police authorities and national health services. The Ministry of Defence is entitled to exclude certain defence goods and services and work involving special security measures.

Types of contracts

All types of commercial contracts for services awarded by a contracting authority are subject to the procurement rules unless they are specifically excepted or the value of the contract falls below financial thresholds which vary according to the type of contract. If the contracts are for works or supplies rather than for services, they will fall to be dealt with under the other parts of the procurement regime as appropriate, so that overlap is avoided, and so that no contract is subject to more than one set of regulations. If a contract is for both goods and services, the value of each part must be calculated and if the value for the services exceeds the value of the goods, the contract will be defined as a services contract.

Exceptions include employment contracts and agreements for arbitration and conciliation services, which do not need to be advertised across the EU. Contracts for IT services, however, do come within the procurement rules.

Threshold values

The Regulations apply only if the value of a services procurement contract will equal or exceed value thresholds. These are intended to confine the number of contracts which are subject to the regime to a number which can be properly monitored and effectively implemented. The values are stated in euros rounded down to the nearest thousand, and also published in the equivalent national currencies of those participating states which have not adopted the single currency. They are converted by using an historic conversion rate based on rates from the previous year.

Generally speaking, the estimated value is the price to be paid for the contract, ignoring VAT. The calculation for the estimated value of an outsourcing contract may be difficult. Where a total price cannot be specified, there are detailed provisions for assessing the value. Rules are laid down to ensure that a single large contract cannot be separated into units so that in isolation each individual contract would be below the limit and thereby avoid the rules. Each contract must be looked at to see if it is in fact one of a series.

Thus, if a number of contracts are awarded at the same time for a single requirement for services, the estimated value of each single contract is counted towards the aggregated value of all of them. Where contracts for particular types of services are regular or renewed, the aggregate value of similar contracts for the same types of services over the previous year adjusted to take account of anticipated changes in quality and costs for the forthcoming year, or the value estimated for the next twelve months or for the whole contract duration, has to be taken into account in order to calculate the threshold. The deemed value of a contract under which services are to be provided to a contracting authority for a fixed period of longer than four years, or indefinitely, is obtained by multiplying the monthly value by 48 – whatever the actual duration of the contract. Where there is an option to terminate the contract after a certain time, the highest amount payable is taken as the value of the contract.

General procedure and notices

In general, under the public procurement regime, contracting authorities must:

- follow specified procedures in seeking offers;
- give notices about the contract in prescribed formats at various stages of the procedures;
- give fair consideration to bidders from anywhere in the EU;
- award the contract according to specified criteria;
- publish details of the award made.

All public notices required in connection with the tendering and award processes by public authorities where the value exceeds the threshold must be publicized in the *Official Journal of the European Union,* the 'Official Journal'. This journal is published every working day in all working languages of the EU. The Official Journal comes in three sections: C – for information and notices; L – which publishes legislation and S – for public procurement invitations to tender.

These advertisements are a means of ensuring that any company who might have an interest in bidding can discover that there is the opportunity of work.

Some companies offer specialist services in scanning the Official Journal on behalf of their clients to select notices which will be of interest to those clients who may wish to make a bid.

The procedure for contracting authorities requires three kinds of notices at various stages: the prior information notice, the contract notice and the award notice. There are standard forms for the publication of notices, each containing specified information.

Prior information notices are published soon after the start of a contracting authority's financial year for the purposes of announcing those services contracts which fall within the regime which it expects to be awarding in that year.

Once a decision is taken to proceed, a *contract notice* gives more information about an individual contract according to which specific procedure is being followed: to invite tenders (the open procedure) or to request interested parties to participate (the restricted procedure or negotiated procedure). Under the negotiated procedure, the notice may be dispensed with in certain circumstances.

The *award notice* is published when the contract has been awarded.

The notices may be transmitted electronically or sent in hard copy. If electronic methods of notification are used and the contract documentation is available on the web, this reduces the minimum timescales allowed.

Procedures for inviting tenders

In inviting tenders and negotiating for the award of individual contracts, the contracting authority must follow one of the defined procedures: open, restricted, negotiated or competitive dialogue.

In principle, either the open or restricted procedure should be followed. The negotiated procedure should be used only exceptionally. The tendering procedure can be avoided altogether only in narrowly defined restricted circumstances such as extreme urgency. There are time limits specified throughout the procedures, consisting in every case of a set number of days during which notices must be published, information supplied and tenders received, in order to provide proper opportunities to interested parties.

Under the *open procedure*, no pre-selection takes place. The invitation is open to all interested parties to submit priced bids. The authority must consider all the tenders received, and select according to the permitted criteria. This is rarely used for IT services.

In the other procedures there is pre-selection of suppliers, who have responded to a prior information notice, who have replied to a contract notice or who are qualified under the rules of the qualification system. The selection must be on the defined objective criteria.

Under the *restricted procedure*, the authority selects certain suppliers to submit tenders out of those who have initially expressed interest in the contract advertised. This permits an early screening process on the basis of such criteria as technical ability and financial standing, and will limit the number of suppliers from amongst whom the final decision must be made. Enough contractors should pass this first selection stage 'to ensure genuine competition', a minimum of five candidates – provided that at least these numbers have responded.

Written invitations to tender must be sent out simultaneously to each of these selected suppliers. Rules detail what documentation goes with the invitation, whether it has to be enclosed with the invitation or whether it can be obtained from a stated address. The shortlisted supplier candidates will be invited to interview or to give presentations to the evaluation panel.

Post-tender negotiation is not permitted except to clarify or supplement the tenders put forward. The successful contractor will be announced, and unsuccessful tenderers must be provided with an explanation of the decision in relation to them, on request.

In either the open or restricted procedure, a tenderer may ask for clarification of the invitation to tender and the information provided with it. All tenderers will be circulated with the replies to ensure that the same information is available to all.

The *negotiated procedure* avoids the time-consuming general competition of the open and restricted procedures, and therefore offers advantages if it can be complied with. Like the restricted procedure, it is a two-stage process. A contract notice must still be published in the Official Journal of the intention to seek offers for a public services contract. A decision is made after consulting with contractors of the contracting authority's choice and considering the results of the consultation.

The negotiated procedure is more relaxed than the other two procedures and is the most limited in application. However, in practice it is used extensively, although a contracting authority has to be able to justify this choice of procedure. The justification may be because tenders received under open or restricted procedures were irregular or unacceptable, or none was received; or because the nature of the contract does not allow prior pricing or a precise specification (this is often the reason the negotiated procedure is followed); or because the contract is for research and development. The negotiated procedure may also sometimes be used without publishing a contract notice, for example in the absence of appropriate tenders in response to an open or restricted procedure; or where for technical, artistic or legal reasons, the contract may only be carried out by a particular contractor.

The advertisement need give only enough information to attract appropriate bidders. The tender documentation will include the detailed specification, which may be refined during the initial period.

The open, restricted and negotiated procedures have been in existence since the public procurement regime was introduced in the early 1990s. The *competitive dialogue procedure* was defined much more recently.[7] It is suitable for complex contracts where the contracting authority can define its overall requirements, but not the best methods of delivery, technical solutions or project structure. Large infrastructure projects are one example of this, and transformational outsourcing projects another. It is a process for dialogue with potential suppliers before bids are submitted. The contracting authority publishes a contract notice, which includes the award criteria, giving a minimum time limit. The criteria may include environmental performance, performance generally, safety and quality assurance. They must not specify makes or processes, nor refer to trade marks, patents or specified production.

At least three potential suppliers are selected to enter into dialogue. This continues until the technical, legal and/or economic solutions are defined. The invitation will consist of all the contract documents, state the deadline for the receipt of tenders, the address, the languages and relative weighting of the criteria. All tenderers must be treated equally, and their information treated in confidence (but only during the procedure). At the end of the dialogue, with a solution identified, the potential suppliers submit their final tenders. Even after this, they may clarify their tenders. The contract is awarded on the basis of the award criteria and the most economically advantageous tender.

The competitive dialogue procedure was intended to facilitate collaboration with the customer in a competitive and commercial context But it has been criticised as 'costly and cumbersome' and for expecting potential suppliers to act as consultants during the procedure.[8]

---

7   The Public Contracts Regulations 2006.
8   David Gollancz 'Lost in translation', *The Lawyer*, 30 January 2006.

Technical specifications

There are rules on setting technical specifications and standards as a requirement for the services to be supplied and the goods and materials associated with the services. They must be based on technical standards, or performance or functional requirements. The broad reasoning behind this is that 'the existence of differing technical regulations and national standards creates a barrier to the free movement of goods and services within the community'. Another main factor intrinsic to IT is to encourage exchange of information, open systems and systems interoperability. Purchasers should not be unnecessarily tied in to suppliers if they are upgrading or enhancing their systems. Contracting authorities must not set standards which could exclude otherwise valid competition, such as standards which are currently promulgated only in the authority's country.

Standards should be specified as a requirement only when it is reasonable to do so. A tender will be valid if it meets the technical specifications in an 'equivalent' way. The UK Office of Government Commerce has issued guidance for public sector agencies to identify requirements in generic terms rather than particular brands or products in their tender documents, except exceptionally, and then to add 'or equivalent'.[9]

Selecting the supplier

The suitability of the tenderer must be assessed in terms of soundness and integrity, economic and financial standing and technical capability. Additional criteria may be specified provided that they are not discriminatory. The only grounds for disqualification of tenderers are where they fall short of the economic, financial or technical standards required.

Thus grounds for disqualification by contracting authorities which are non-discriminatory and therefore permitted include, not surprisingly, the supplier's insolvency or gross misconduct; its reputation; professional qualifications; economic standing; and technical knowledge and ability. Suppliers must be excluded if their directors or other senior decision makers have been convicted of fraud or corruption.

The only grounds on which to award a public services contract are either that the tender is the most economically advantageous to the authority, or that it is the lowest priced. These are not necessarily the same. The former criterion

---

9   http://www.ogc.gov.uk.

allows factors other than price to be considered, such as 'value for money', quality, technical merit. These factors have to be relatively weighted, in the notice to prospective tenderers or supplied as part of the documentation. Factors which are not listed may not be taken into account. A tender which is the lowest price but abnormally low for the transaction concerned may be rejected, although an explanation should be sought before it is disqualified. A report that this has occurred has to be sent to the European Commission.

Notice will be published in the Official Journal either that an award has been made or the reason why it has not been made.

Complaints about awards

An unsuccessful tenderer is entitled to be informed as soon as possible of the successful tender. Unsuccessful suppliers will have invested time and money in bidding and are entitled to see that the process has been fair. This should be helpful to contractors in a practical way for their future tender strategy. However, they may also review the reasons given to consider whether there is any legal redress.

An EC Directive on remedies[10] has introduced a mandatory standstill period of ten or fifteen days (according to whether the notification was electronic, by fax or by post) between the contract award and entering into the contract. This gives unsuccessful tenderers an opportunity of seeking review of the decision before the award goes ahead. If the contracting authority does not comply with the notification process requirements or the standstill period, the contract is deemed to have been illegally awarded and is open to challenge.

Other rules deriving from EC Directives set out procedures for lodging a complaint against contracting authorities, and detailing the remedies available if the procedures are not followed.[11]

Unsuccessful tenderers based in the EU who have genuine cause for complaint over the selection procedures, have remedies through the courts directly against contracting authorities and utilities who do not comply with the public procurement obligations. For example, a supplier may believe it would have won the procurement process had it been properly conducted, or may believe it was unfairly excluded from bidding.

---

10   EC Public Procurement Remedies Directive 2007/66/EC.
11   The Compliance Directive (89/665/EEC).

Damages can be awarded against a contracting authority that fails to comply with the procurement regime. If the contract has been awarded, an aggrieved supplier who believes that it has suffered loss as a result of a breach of the procurement rules – in practice because it has not obtained a contract that it believes it should have – and who can quantify the loss it consequently suffers, may claim damages against the contracting authority concerned through the courts if the procedure was not complied with or the contract has been unfairly awarded to another party. The court must assess whether the supplier would have been awarded the contract had the proper procedures been followed. That would form the basis for damages, as potential loss of profit. It could be that the only direct loss would be the cost of tendering and that anything else is too speculative. For a supplier who was not in a position to tender because it did not know about the contract, the damages would be even more difficult to assess.

An action must be brought promptly, and in any event within three months of the date the grounds first arose, unless the court extends that time limit by reason of exceptional circumstances.

The European Commission is itself entitled to take action to enforce the Directives within member states, and a supplier may alternatively make a complaint to the European Commission. This is confidential and avoids legal costs. However, this is not a means for the supplier to obtain damages, because the Commission brings actions against member states rather than the defaulting contracting authority.

Conclusion

The intention of the public procurement regime is to encourage competition in order to bring ultimate cost savings to public authorities. The legal requirements and basic contract terms must be considered at the outset of outsourcing.

Involvement in the selection process can be expensive, both for customers who have to prepare documentation and weigh up the merits of different tenderers, and for tenderers who have to respond to enquiries and submit proposals, many of which need to be fairly comprehensive.

Both the European Commission and the UK Government keep the operation of competition and fairness in public sector procurement under review.

The view has been expressed that the public sector handles outsourcing procurement better than the private sector. The initial procurement stage ensures effective competitive leverage, and sufficient resources are devoted to managing and overseeing the project within the public sector than in private business. This means that the procedure takes longer but the processes are better understood to provide a stable outsourcing transaction.[12]

---

12 Alistair Maugham, *Stop Laughing and Start Learning from Public Sector Outsourcing*, silicon.com, 2 May 2003, http://comment.silicon.com/0,39024711,10003991,00.htm.

Services and Service Level Agreements

An outsourcing contract is defined by reference to the services which are being contracted out. The customer is paying for the provision of services by the supplier according to agreed standards, the service levels. The ongoing assessment of the success of the contract will be by the process of overseeing and reviewing the standards of service which are achieved in practice. Rebates or payments may be made by the supplier to the customer in the event of failure of services to achieve key service levels.

One of the most important parts of the contract will therefore be about the services and service levels. The supplier will give a commitment to provide the specified services, and associated with this obligation will be a further undertaking to provide the services according to the service levels.

The services and the service levels required will be unique to the customer organization. Although the services being outsourced by two different organizations may be apparently similar, the substantive details, relative priorities and performance criteria for one company may well be irrelevant for the other. Moreover, over time and with experience in working with them, it is highly probable that the services and service levels initially agreed will change. The opportunity for revision should be built into the contract.

For business transformation services, the scope will need to be carefully defined, but service levels may be less precise, or their definition be subject to more frequent review than is usually the case.

This chapter focuses on the services to be performed and their associated service levels. For business transformation services, the scope will need to be defined equally carefully, but the detailed requirements will be specified in terms which allow for flexibility and more specific review procedures.

Services

The services to be provided should be described in the contract in terms of their scope, the extent of the supplier's management responsibilities in relation to them, and how much flexibility is to be allowed for in the case of any additional services required. The customer may be able to include a sweep-up clause for other services not specifically defined, which will be useful in ensuring that everything can come under the outsourcing umbrella. However, a supplier should beware of generic open-ended statements of its service obligations over and above the services which have been originally listed.

The first general statements identifying the services should set out the primary obligations of the supplier: what the services are for, whether this is a statement about management of operational data processing, or networks or help desks, for selective outsourcing, or a general statement that the services comprise the whole IT capability. The committed time within which the services are to be provided should be clear; is it to be round the clock, every day of the year, or some lesser availability? The location of the processing or the destination of the outputs may be specified. The supplier may be undertaking to run efficient systems for tracking and managing problems and changes; to co-ordinate operations and procedures with the customer, end users, other suppliers; generally to comply with service levels. Capacity planning, security management, training and quality control may also be considered as part of the services provided by the supplier. Resilience (core facilities, degraded service, recovery and so on) must be addressed. These or other responsibilities may be allocated between the supplier and customer. Who is to ensure that documentation is up to date and who controls its circulation? Will the supplier want to exclude responsibility for data preparation, or for faults on input made by the customer or by a third party? Who is in charge of job control and scheduling? Who controls the maintenance and renewal of equipment at the customer's or end user's premises?

These are the sorts of initial questions which may need to be asked.

SERVICES

- How are the services defined?

Category	Examples
Business area	Purchasing, Finance, Production, Sales
Type of service	Operations, Development, Administration, Management, Maintenance and Support, Security
System	Order Processing, Credit Control, Call Centre
Operation	On-line, Mainframe, Distributed

For the scope of the services, are the following relevant for each particular service?

QUALITY ASSURANCE AND STANDARDS

- What inspection, testing requirements, and sign-off procedures will be required (for the system development life cycle in particular)?

- Is formal compliance with quality control and quality assurance required?

- ISO/IEC 20000 is the standard for IT service management.[1] It consists of two parts:

  - ISO/IEC 20000-1: 2005, defining the requirements for delivery of managed services.

  - ISO/IEC 20000-2: 2005, which assists organizations being audited on delivery of managed services or who are deciding on improvements to services.

  An organization may gain certification to ISO/IEC 20000 criteria through third party audit and assessment. The IT Service Management Forum[2] ('*it*SMF') created and manages the related IT Service Management Certification scheme. It is a member association for industry best practice and professionalism in IT Service Management. The members may be large or small organizations in both the public and the private sector, or individual consultants.

- Are codes of conduct or codes of practice for staff to be included?

SERVICE HOURS

- Will the services all be carried out during normal working hours (which should be defined)?

---

1   http://www.isoiec20000certification.com/.
2   http://www.itsmf.co.uk.

- Is there to be provision for extending normal working hours on notice?

- Are public holidays, weekends and overtime ever to be allowed for, as a matter of course, or only if the customer gives advance notice (and how much notice)?

- Are certain times and availabilities more important than others, for example, tax year end, daily close of business?

- Are there strict deadlines?

- How will emergencies be catered for?

- Do the time scales depend on the inputs being received by a certain time?

VOLUMES AND CAPACITIES

- Average, typical, maximum and frequencies;

- Anticipated growth;

- Actual and target availability;

- Will any of the service levels depend on external lines of supply? If so, the commitment must be backed up in the contracts with the third parties concerned.

EXCLUSIONS

- What is to be allowed for as scheduled unavailability – for equipment maintenance, implementation of new software, installation of new equipment, building servicing, staff training, for example? Can this be carried out during normal working hours or will the customer pay the extra costs of overtime?

MAINTENANCE AND SUPPORT

- Maintenance – preventive and remedial;

- Who is responsible for supplying and maintaining peripherals and operational consumables, such as magnetic tapes, discs and cartridges?

- Recovery times for unscheduled service outages.

HELP DESK

- What response times are expected for the initial acknowledgment of queries and problems?

- Will they be categorized by priority?

- How long should it take to solve a problem?

- Is there an escalation procedure for more resources to be committed to finding a solution?

SYSTEM DEVELOPMENT SERVICES

- Can performance requirements be identified at this stage for business analysis, feasibility studies, package selection, specification and design?

- How far is the supplier expected to take the initiative in identifying business opportunities for new technology or systems?

EDUCATION AND TRAINING

- What are the proposals for training new end users and new employees of the supplier?

BACK UP ARRANGEMENTS

- Are there adequate contingency planning and disaster recovery procedures?

Defining the service levels

Service levels demonstrate the performance of 'reasonable skill and care' and are the key to a successful outsourcing relationship. They are the specification of mutually acceptable, measurable standards of performance by the supplier, which are agreed to be reasonably attainable under normal circumstances in practice. They should not be merely optimistic targets to aim for hopefully.

Some provisions will be implied at law into a contract, whether or not they are actually expressly worded. Under legislation covering the supply of services, a term is implied into all contracts for services that the services will be carried out with reasonable skill and care within a reasonable time.[3] The definition of 'reasonable' depends on the circumstances, and it is therefore more practical

---

3   Supply of Goods and Services Act 1982.

for both parties that the supplier should give precise commitments about skill, care and time frames.

Measuring the service levels

As part of the process of compiling the service levels, decisions need to be made on how much time and energy should be devoted to measuring them. There are automated techniques available for measuring some processes, and a combination of manual and automated systems will be used.

The emphasis in drawing up the service levels should be on deliverables, not processes – on ends, not means. In principle, the customer should not be concerned with the methods of delivery. For example, it may not matter to the customer how often a process has to be run to produce a result, if the service level target of a report produced within a time limit is met. In some cases, particular procedures may need to be followed, (for example, to ensure compatibility between two systems or to satisfy the requirements of particular end users, or where they are directly related to the method of charging) but this should be regarded as an exception. It is normally the supplier's responsibility to decide how the objectives in the outsourcing are to be reached. If the customer stresses certain procedures or techniques, this could hamper an innovative supplier from finding different and more efficient routes to achieving the objectives.

All key services must be measurable. This may be straightforward when response times, transaction completion times or volumes are concerned. However, some activities will be required as part of the services without operational damage actually resulting if they are not met. A supplier may claim to have high standards of courtesy, but levels of politeness are a subjective matter and not easily measurable in terms which both parties would be happy to accept. It may be a service requirement for the supplier's staff to dress appropriately, but it would not bring a system crashing down if a failure occurred, even if the existence of the failure could be agreed. There may be exceptions to this, perhaps for staff who meet the public as part of their work.

'Customer satisfaction' always provides room for argument. It may be important – particularly if the supplier makes promotional claims of its abilities in this direction. If necessary, acceptable criteria must be agreed by both sides, but will probably be largely subjective. It will not be readily amenable to enforcement by means of the normal incentives to performance discussed below. Questionnaires for end users may be devised, offering responses in the form of numerical values to cover timeliness of information provided, quality of service, value for money and staff attitudes. Shortcomings which arise may have to be addressed through management procedures.

A bland undertaking to keep 'supplying the service previously supplied' is unlikely to be acceptable, worded as generally as this, although this principle may be a good starting point (but not necessarily, if the main reason for outsourcing is to improve the service).

A commitment by the supplier to guarantee '98 per cent availability' is equally unsatisfactory. It is open to various interpretations. What is the 'availability' to cover, and what does '98 per cent' mean? Is it actually a service where anything less than 100 per cent cannot be tolerated? For example, one breach of security may be one too many. Or, as is more likely, is a graduated failure pattern to be measured? There may be a general level of acceptability for a daily report to be produced within an agreed number of hours, and failures to an agreed level could accumulate to the point at which they are unacceptable over the defined period. Some of the services will be important only at particular times. Are there points at which failure is critical, for the month-end run, or at end-of-year?

Thus measurement should be accurately defined and realistic. Can it be related to existing meaningful time parameters, the periods between meetings, or accounting periods? Should this be consistently 98 per cent during working hours, and within a 'month'? Further precision is necessary. Is it to be a calendar month, or a rolling four-week period?

A service period may be measured as a precise band of time – such as a number of consecutive weeks, starting at 6 am on the first Monday where processing is continuous. The services can then be measured in terms of availability, response times, number of faults, time to repair. Measurement may be by sampling. Where there are levels which fluctuate, the problem is whether to take the best or the worst examples. There must be clear criteria for sampling if there are known to be wide fluctuations in performance.

The supplier must be able to meet the service level requirements even if resources are temporarily inadequate because of holidays, illness, resignations, equipment breakdowns or external failures.

In some cases service levels will be dependent on actions taken by the customer or third parties. This must be specified, for example, 'subject to the input data being received by noon on Day One, the report will be available by 9 am on Day Two'.

Charges are often explicitly linked to service level performance. In any case there is a direct relationship between the cost of the outsourcing contract and the levels of service which are acceptable. The ideal for the customer is error-free performance one hundred per cent of the time. However, the cost of supplying this service overall, even if it were practically attainable, will normally be out of the question, although there may be specific exceptions for certain elements of the services. The service levels represent what the customer is prepared to afford. The higher the level of service required, the less the margin of error which will be acceptable, and the more expensive the outsourcing will be.

It is important for both sides that the supplier should recognise the quality of service expected by the customer. It is up to both parties to assess what is realistic, balancing cost against quality. The customer must decide what it will pay. The supplier must be satisfied that the service can be delivered profitably.

Existing service level measurements

Some customer organizations will already be measuring the services provided by the existing IT department. They may have quality assurance throughout the organization, perhaps if they have critical manufacturing processes for which precision is required in their business. In this event, the basic information will already be available for drawing up the service level agreements, and the task will be more easily manageable and take less time than having to start from scratch.

Indeed, one good way of preparing early for the prospect of outsourcing is for the customer to take the initiative in drawing up service levels well before the invitation to tender is issued. This in itself has been known on the one hand to improve responsiveness to end users by the IT department, and on the other, to create new expectations by the end users of what is sensibly achievable. Thus by enabling greater understanding of the role and functions of the IT department it may even help to ameliorate a political situation within an organization. It will also furnish a benchmark for comparison of what the IT department can offer as against external tenders. Of course, a possible side effect would be to obviate the need for outsourcing.

If the supplier has to take the customer's existing figures, it will need to analyse the service level metrics and their history itself. Is there a record of consistency? The supplier needs to know whether the service levels have consistently been achieved and that the figures have been used in management control, over the period prior to the negotiations, normally at least the previous twelve months prior to contract signature.

The customer may be asked to warrant the service levels if the supplier has no means of independently checking their accuracy. This is not a meaningful warranty and should be resisted. How could it be disproved?

The supplier may be able to suggest improvements to any existing service levels. This will set the scene for a more cost-effective outsourcing relationship for the customer.

Agreeing the service levels

If there are no existing measures, or if current services are not meeting expectations, time will need to be spent by both parties in determining the service levels, ideally before the contract is signed. This may be an unattainable counsel of perfection in the actual situation. The initial exercise of producing the service level agreements will not always be completed by the time the outsourcing contract comes into effect, for various reasons.

Defining the service levels could be undertaken as a joint exercise or the supplier may use its own experience in outsourcing, and build on the knowledge it has gained in making its tender by carrying out the exercise. It may seek to impose a charge for this work.

If it is necessary to take the outsourcing ahead before the service levels have been defined to the satisfaction of both parties, one way of dealing with the situation is to have temporary arrangements at the start of the outsourcing, perhaps based on average performance levels currently being achieved in the business, and to finalize the requirements during a transitional period after the contract has been signed and the outsourcing process introduced, during which the services will be measured in order to set sustainable service levels, before a given deadline or cutover point.

Where any service levels are stated as 'to be agreed', this must be followed up at the project review meetings and noted, and dates for finalizing them should be set as targets. 'Agreements to agree' are not definite enough to be legally enforceable, but will state the common intention in an area where it is in the interests of both parties to have the service levels clarified eventually.

This is not to be recommended, but sometimes there is no other way. It should not be considered as either a typical or a satisfactory way of short-circuiting the negotiating process in order to get the contract signed. If possible a procedure should be prescribed for agreeing the limits of the service levels with a fixed timetable and with resort to a special form of dispute resolution which should be laid down in the contract, to be invoked for any difficulties which arise in connection with the definition of service levels during this transitional period.

In whatever ways the exercise in setting service levels is carried out, both the supplier and the user must approve the results.

There should be some scope for flexibility. It will not automatically be possible to define all the service levels correctly at once, or to guarantee that they will remain the same if the business context and technology should change. Moreover, the risk of the slow decline of service levels during the contract term should be recognized.

The services themselves and their service levels should therefore be reviewed regularly to evaluate their continuing benefit. The supplier may be expected to provide additional or revised services if so required by the customer, subject to agreeing any further charges to be imposed, as part of the scope for varying the contract. New service levels may have to be agreed. The structure for meetings and the reports produced should facilitate the discussions and enable implementation of any updates or changes, under the variation procedures discussed in Chapter 10.

Respective roles in performance assessment

During the outsourcing, the supplier will be responsible for keeping the performance statistics. Automated processes will help maintain the statistics. Computer systems and software and other equipment such as telecommunications equipment and network monitors, can provide much information as to usage and performance. This information will be passed to the customer, in an agreed format which should be documented in the contract, normally by the provision of written reports within a number of days after the end of each time period, for review at the progress meetings. For simple processes, a form of exception reporting may be acceptable. It will form part of the review process at the management meetings, discussed further in Chapter 9. Both the customer and the supplier will be responsible for ensuring that the standards are maintained, with the supplier's obligation to observe them and the customer's right to check them.

Other statistics must be kept and reviewed from time to time to note whether the service levels in general are working successfully, whether an improved service would be feasible, and how future requirements will impact the existing services.

Incentives for performance

Once the service levels have been ascertained, the impact of failure to meet them must be assessed and the consequences defined in the contract. This can entail considerable negotiation. They must be acceptable to both parties.

It is important that any failures are resolved quickly before they become accepted. There are many stages of remedying defective performance before resorting to the worst sanction of termination of the contract. This is a remedy to be invoked only when all else has failed. At that point the customer will be in an unenviable position.

If service levels are not being attained, it follows that there is a failure by the supplier in complying with the terms of the contract. As a result the customer is getting less than has been agreed to be provided for the charges payable, and should consequently not have to pay the full amount.

The supplier may therefore be required to make payments or accept a remission in the charges if performance for critical services is below what has been agreed and yet the situation is redeemable so that termination of the contract would not be a necessary or desirable option.

Service credits, sometimes known as performance index rebates, and liquidated damages are the two approaches to this. Alternatively suppliers sometimes offer to provide additional services without charge as compensation. This suits them well in working ever more closely with the customer. Yet the customer will not be recompensed if the services provided are no improvement on the original failures to meet the targets.

Service credits, linked to critical service failures singly or in combination, represent a simple form of price adjustment for not achieving the contracted-for service. Liquidated damages are a form of compensation estimated in advance, denoting the foreseeable financial loss to the customer of breach of contract, in this case of more serious failure to provide specific services to particular levels. The principles of liquidated damages are discussed further in Chapter 13.

However, in outsourcing, financial recompense to the customer for the supplier's failure to meet the service levels while the contract continues in force is intended primarily to be a financial incentive for the supplier to maintain or improve the service levels by a threat of reduction in profits, rather than to be comprehensive compensation for the customer.

Service credits may be payable as fixed sums or treated as rebates to the charges. Liquidated damages will normally be expressed in terms of a sum or as a percentage or fraction related, for example, to a daily rate or other rate on which the charges are based, by adjustment to the charges payable or by cash payment by the supplier to the customer. If actual money is being paid out by the supplier, then terms of payment should be set out in the contract.

For example, liquidated damages may be payable for unavailability over a period of time of a particular critical service or constantly degraded response times. Service credits may be payable in respect of failure of individual measured services.

In practice, the distinction between service credits and liquidated damages can become blurred.

An overall performance index may be constructed as a technique for prioritising the critical services and calculating the amounts due. First, an analysis of the services to identify the key activities crucial to the customer's business success will be necessary. The approach should be to focus on those measures which really matter, that are quantifiable and objectively measurable over defined time periods, such as accounting periods or on a monthly basis. Some services may be accrued over different business units, or by site. A sample number of critical processes may be taken as being representative.

One method of proceeding is to draw up a worksheet for each vital service – or system or business function or product, according to how the service levels are categorized and defined.

- Set out on the worksheet the function of that service, and its impact on the overall business operation.

- Specify on the worksheet, and if possible quantify, the consequences of failure to reach the agreed service levels, taking into account any measures that would be pragmatically taken by the customer to minimise the extent of the lack of performance. For example, if the help-line telephone line were out of action for a number of hours through the supplier's failure, an alternative telephone number could be established. All the users would have to be notified of the new telephone number and re-notified when the original line is restored. Could the resource time of doing this be quantified and evaluated?

• Show the calculations on the worksheet for the costs involved for internal purposes, as a reminder for the customer of the justification behind the figures.

• Agree an aggregate figure for the supplier to make available overall within any one year, rolling twelve months or other time frame, to be applied for rebates, remission of charges or actual payment.

• This total figure will depend on the perceived level of risk, the basis of the charges and the profitability of the contract to the supplier. This figure should be enough to act as an inducement for the supplier to restore performance, without being of such magnitude that it would in itself wreck the supplier's profit margins and create the risk of insolvency. Taking an extreme hypothetical position, if all the critical services failed to their fullest extent accumulated over the period concerned, the total remission obtainable would be limited to this maximum sum. Of course, what would actually happen before this catastrophe occurred is that the disaster recovery procedures would have been implemented and various other practical measures taken, because in this doomsday scenario, if nothing else happened, the customer would no longer be operating a viable business, and such a major failure would justifiably threaten the supplier's solvency. However, for incentive purposes, this is how the payments are worked out.

• Break down this amount by allocation among the critical performance standards, weighted according to their relative value.

• This allocation is an artificial mechanism which may be based on formulae of greater or less complexity. For example, a weighting may be applied in calculating rebates payable in respect of any individual critical service in terms of its relative value to the others, or to some benchmark. Response times for a particularly important online process might have been given a weighting of 20 per cent compared with a weighting of 1 per cent for speed of responses to a database enquiry system. It follows in this example that the first process is regarded in that organization as twenty times more important than the second, which is far less critical, and that this would be reflected in the respective rebates proposed for failure of these particular services. The accumulated values of the rebates together form a weighted performance index.

Some allowance will normally be made to breaches of service levels before payments or rebates are triggered. Thus, this may take the form of:

- an achieved service level being less than the agreed service level by a set percentage before the service credit falls due;

- the rolling period over which the performance is measured may be greater than a single time period;

- unavailability of a service over a limited period of time;

- an accumulated number of service level failures within a number of hours or within a single time period;

- a distinction being drawn between minor and major variances to performance level. For minor variances, the parties will agree corrective action within a given time scale. If this does not lead to restoration of the agreed performance level, it automatically becomes a significant variance. A number of minor variances, or a single or small number of major variances, may therefore trigger a service credit in the accounting period concerned.

The supplier may argue that following payment or remission or rebate, the failure record should be cleared and the accumulation will restart. This may mean that over time unsatisfactory service levels are being maintained without being so bad as to trigger incentive payments. Consequently there may need to be a single incentive to raise the general level of performance. This could be formally reviewed less frequently that the normal measurement periods, perhaps at the end of each year, and a sum set aside as remission to cover accumulated poor performance of this nature.

A failure or loss of service which occurs because of events outside the supplier's control and therefore not reasonably attributable to the supplier should be specifically excluded in the contract from the calculations for performance incentives. This is known as *force majeure* and is discussed at greater length in Chapter 13.

For loss of some services, it will not be possible to set a calculated, objective figure, and yet for the purposes of motivation, a small sum might be allowed as recognition of recompense. Thus, if a proportion of the charges are made for desktop maintenance, in a particular installation lack of maintenance might have to extend to a large number of machines to have any critical operational impact. A service credit might then be agreed if the failure to maintain were to exceed a certain time period or number of machines in spite of the lack of quantifiable estimated loss.

Either service credits or liquidated damages may be selected for any particular failure, or they can operate together. If they are both to be included there should be a contractual provision to prevent them accumulating at the same time to create a double recovery in respect of a single ground of fault.

In addition to these payment criteria being invoked, the supplier should contractually commit to taking corrective action. Measures to address the source of the inadequate performance will be the primary action. Consideration may need to be given by both parties to changing the service levels and/or the prices if the implication is that there is a reduction in services.

There may also be a definition of 'material breach' if sufficient failures occur or if a single failure lasts for longer than a specified time, to entitle the customer to terminate the contract if the service level failures are so serious that this becomes necessary.

While service credits and liquidated damages are being negotiated, a supplier may seek a bonus as positive motivation for exceeding service levels. But the customer is paying for those service levels it requires for its business. There will normally be no commercial benefit to the customer in enhanced service levels, or if there is, it will be an unlooked for, even unnecessary, benefit for which the customer will not expect to have to pay.

The compensation criteria must be relatively simple to administer. Otherwise the problems of invoking them will detract from all the time and effort put into drawing up the service levels and key performance indicators. One non-financial incentive which may be considered for inclusion in the contract for implementing when there is a failure to meet service levels, is to require a senior named director or manager from the supplier to visit the customer and explain to the customer's counterpart what has happened and what is being done to correct matters.

Contractual documentation

If there is a large number or variety of services, they may be catalogued in a separate schedule in a document which is referenced from the services clause in the main body of the agreement. This will also be the most efficient way of allowing for an expansion of service provision during the life of the contract, as the schedule can be amended without affecting the agreement itself.

The service levels themselves and the formulae used in establishing them will also normally be in a separate document, or in several such documents, being the service level agreements, which will be formally incorporated into the contract to be integral to it and legally enforceable.

The definitions of the services and service levels should be reviewed from a legal point of view. The wording should be unambiguous and readily understandable, and the requirements should be set out clearly. Tables and matrices may be appropriate.

The financial principles according to which the service credits or liquidated damages become payable are also normally articulated separately, as another schedule. This document must be related to the services and the service level agreements.

The format of the documents should facilitate amendments, enhancements, additions and deletions. There should be a front page for document change control, noting the dates and issue numbers of amendments and circulation. It may be helpful for each page to be dated and given an issue number.

The service level agreement should be a working document during the life of the contract and essential for ongoing reference in order to monitor performance. The documents must be made available to those people who are responsible for meeting the service levels, so that they know what is required.

Business Assets: Premises and Equipment

Special considerations arise in those outsourcing arrangements where the customer's assets are to become the responsibility of the supplier. In this chapter some of the principal factors which will require attention in respect of premises and equipment are discussed. Software is considered in Chapter 7.

All outsourcing contracts are about the services which are to be carried out for the customer by the supplier to agreed standards. Some outsourcing transactions extend beyond this. In those cases where the customer is handing over a large part of its IT capability or the whole of its IT function for the supplier to run, the hardware, other equipment and assets used will be transferred to the supplier to use in the provision of the services. The supplier may acquire the customer's premises in order to continue to carry out the services. In such circumstances, the outsourcing contract must therefore cover the legal issues involved in transferring the assets associated with the services from the customer to the supplier's control.

If premises are to be transferred from the customer to the supplier by sale, lease or licence in order to carry out the outsourcing, various specialist services will be required, in addition to commercial property law advice. Specialized financial advice will undoubtedly be beneficial in relation to the price being paid in connection with the business transfer. The timing, allocation and apportionment of sums among the different categories of what is being transferred and the extent of any pre-payments, will be significant for taxation purposes, such as corporation tax and value added tax, and a taxation law adviser will be able to assist. Local advice may be necessary for a multi-national outsourcing. If the outsourcing is second or third generation, both the new supplier and customer will need to negotiate with the current supplier about the assets to be transferred from the current supplier.

Not all outsourcing contracts will involve any business transfer features. The services can be carried out at the customer's premises on the customer's equipment, or located at the supplier's site with the supplier's existing hardware and communication systems. In other contracts, arrangements in relation to premises and computer equipment will be an integral part of the transaction.

Business transfer

If there is to be only a limited transfer of assets of the business involved, such as items of simple equipment, the details may be stipulated within one single outsourcing contract document. However, it will be more manageable to create separate but related contractual documents if the transfer of business assets is in any way complex and therefore a significant part of the transaction. The Services Agreement will focus on the continuing outsourcing services. The Business Transfer Agreement will cover the transfer of the assets.

The Business Transfer Agreement will state the prices to be paid in respect of the assets: those which can be sold by the customer to the supplier, the leased interests, and the third party contracts, intellectual property licences, consumable stocks such as paper and forms, and records relating to the outsourced business activities. Certain assets will be specifically excluded: some records and other third party contracts, any book debts, sums to be recovered and some retained assets.

On the agreed date, formal delivery will take place of the assets themselves and the executed agreements. Costs will be allocated to the customer before the cutover date and to the supplier afterwards, and apportioned as necessary for any period extending before and after that date.

The associated contracts falling under the overall aegis of the Business Transfer Agreement are concerned with transfer of various kinds of assets from the customer to the supplier: the property leases, hire contracts, assignments, novations, licences and insurances. The business assets which are owned by third parties, other than the accommodation, may be transferred to the customer by assignment or novation of existing agreements. The differences between assignment and novation are discussed in Chapter 1.

Third parties will not have the same commercial incentives or involvement as the customer and supplier have in progressing the transfer of the agreements with any urgency, where their consent or participation is called for. There is no reason to assume that all existing third party contracts with the customer are satisfactory. The supplier will have to examine the contents of these agreements systematically before taking them over. As to which of the parties should take prime responsibility for getting the consents and licences concerned in the transfers, from landlords, equipment lessors and others, this will largely depend on the supplier's experience in negotiating with third parties on outsourcing-related transfers. It may be that the customer will be in possession of all the relevant information and in a better position to take or keep control. There may be confidentiality obligations requiring the customer to do so initially. In any event, the customer should be prepared to give an undertaking to act reasonably with regard to the existing contracts, and to assist the supplier as necessary in the transfers, perhaps with reimbursement of expenses incurred by the supplier. Agreement must be reached as to who will pay for any costs of obtaining consent from third parties, and what is to be done if the consent is legitimately refused. It may take considerable time and much persuasion to sort matters out acceptably.

The customer will be expected to inform and consult with the supplier during the negotiations, to give assurances about the condition and ownership of those assets it is treating as its own. At the same time it will limit its liability.

Other contracts which the Business Transfer Agreement may address will be those between the customer and third party end users of the services to be outsourced. The end users may be other legal entities within the customer's group of companies or independent companies, who still wish, or need, to take those services.

It may sometimes be practicable for the contract to be activated in stages. There may have been pressures to sign the contract by a particular date, whether for reasons of timing in order to meet an imposed deadline, or for financial or political imperatives, with cutover being deferred for a period. If so, these somewhat imperfect circumstances may allow a timeframe for those who are in charge of co-ordinating the negotiations to confirm all the linked contracts and sort out the service levels prior to cutover. Alternatively a transitional period of weeks or months may follow the formal takeover before the date from which the contract becomes fully effective. It is often during this transitional phase that a number of outstanding issues are finalized.

If the contract is brought into effect in stages, it must be made conditional upon success in reaching agreement on all the outstanding matters and subject to getting all the third party contracts, licences and consents agreed. If any significant element fails to fall into place, it would be normal for the customer to expect to be able to terminate the contract without being obliged to compensate the supplier. However, failure in concluding the collateral agreements may be primarily attributable to the fault of the customer. In this case, negotiations may focus on the amount of compensation which would reasonably be payable to the supplier, and the contract should set out what is expressly agreed.

Premises

The outsourced services may be carried out at the supplier's premises or at the customer's premises, or at both in combination. If the services are to be performed at the customer's existing premises, the site may remain under the customer's control or, as part of the transaction, the supplier may take over the tenancy by licence or lease or ownership of the premises, by purchase. Although property issues should be peripheral to the objective of the outsourcing, it is possible for them to affect the structure and value of the transaction substantially, depending on their value and how they influence the charges to be agreed, and therefore the requirements should be carefully assessed.

If the site is to be sold to the supplier, then the right of the supplier to occupy the premises will continue independently of the outsourcing contract. On termination of the contract for any reason, the supplier will remain in ownership or possession. There will be tax liabilities and consequences to be taken into account, which may affect how the price is to be paid.

Alternatively the site may be leased to the supplier, to give the supplier exclusive rights to use the premises, or it may be licensed, and the supplier may be sharing parts of the site with the customer. For a licence, the supplier will not have exclusive access.

A separate property contract will be negotiated if the supplier will be exclusively using, renting or buying the premises, giving the supplier a legal interest, whether by sale, formal lease or sub-lease, or licence, for the purposes of providing the services. The terms must be negotiated, together with the sale price or rental or other charges. There will be a number of technical matters to work through, with the assistance of property lawyers. For example, the customer must ensure that the supplier does not inadvertently gain security of tenure.

In the case of assignment of the lease or a sub-lease, or where a licence is being granted and the customer is not the freeholder, consent from the original or current lessor to the lease or licence must be obtained – assuming that the terms of the lease will allow the customer to grant a sub-lease or licence. Any existing disputes between the customer and the landlord will give the landlord the opportunity of imposing conditions before granting its consent, and further assessing the desirability of having the supplier as a tenant, according to its financial stability and other relevant characteristics. It may take time for the landlord to grant consent.

Responsibility for the outgoings must be agreed. If the supplier is to have exclusive use of the premises, then it will be responsible for outgoings in respect of upkeep, insurance and maintenance. Heating, air-conditioning, electricity, physical security and cleaning are ongoing costs. Will the cost of these services be directly charged back to the customer, or have they been allowed for in the supplier's charges? If the services are to be provided at the customer's location and the site will remain under the customer's control, the customer will remain responsible for the outgoings.

Who is to be responsible for the security and insurance of the premises and for providing office furniture, equipment and telephone lines?

If the premises are shared, the supplier should ascertain whether its staff will be able to use the general facilities available to the customer's employees, such as canteens and meeting rooms. The customer is entitled to insist that the supplier's staff will comply with security, health and safety regulations. There may be special rules about access and identity cards, or limits on the times during which access is permitted. Regulations may extend to standards of dress and of conduct. These matters should be articulated in the contract.

Business assets

All the assets forming part of the transaction, including computer hardware and communications equipment, third party contracts and software licences, and possibly miscellaneous items such as furniture and consumables, must be identified by listing or describing them, for the Business Transfer Agreement. Those assets which might have been part of the transfer, but which are not included, should also be catalogued if there may be any doubt about them, to clarify the boundaries of what has been agreed.

To say that all the assets must be identified is a simple statement to make. However, problems may arise if accurate and complete information is not already available, such as an asset register. The customer may be required to give a warranty that its asset register is up-to-date.

A range of options in respect of asset transfer will be open to the customer in the outsourcing transaction. Different arrangements for transfer will follow, according to whether the hardware items and other equipment – mainframes, PCs, workstations, communications hardware, servers, etc. – are owned or leased by the customer, and depending on whether particular assets are to be sold, leased or licensed to the supplier.

Some items may simply be sold. The supplier will become responsible for upgrades and replacements for these. The customer will receive an immediate benefit if payment is made at the outset of the arrangement, even if the cost to the supplier is to be recovered as part of the supplier's ongoing charges. There may be tax implications to consider. Whether the outsourcing agreement is terminated early or expires, the customer may need an option to purchase back the same or equivalent items if they will still be needed in providing the services, at a nominal amount (since the price paid to the customer will have been recovered through the charges it will have paid). Again there may be tax implications. If the supplier owns these items and becomes insolvent during the term of the outsourcing contract, and if they are key to the services, this will be yet another of the many problems that would arise for the customer on the supplier's insolvency.

For those assets which are leased, the terms of the lease must be reviewed. It is likely that formal consents or licences will be needed from the lessors for transfer or assignment, or for the agreements to be novated by replacing the customer as party to the original agreement by the supplier. In these circumstances, although the lessors must be approached, they will have no incentive to be positively helpful or to make swift progress, and may need to be encouraged or badgered. The customer may lease its own equipment to the supplier, for the term of the contract. The supplier should maintain an asset register for such items of equipment and will be bound to return it on termination or expiry. A loan to the supplier by way of licence from the customer would be simpler.

Before assets are transferred, the supplier should undertake a process of 'due diligence', closely examining those contracts entered into by the customer in respect of the assets, together with any connected procedures, in order to identify risks and potential future costs. Charges which may arise might be indirect or otherwise not obvious. For example, in relation to insurance costs which will become the responsibility of the supplier, the customer may previously have been able to obtain discount rates as a subsidiary of a larger group through bulk buying, or it may previously have self insured.

The ownership of the equipment may remain with the customer, who must then decide who is to manage it.

The supplier may take over the management, including responsibility for agreeing maintenance and insurance arrangements with third parties.

If the customer remains responsible for the equipment, then consent may be obtained for ancillary maintenance contracts to remain in the customer's name, the customer therefore remaining party to the contract and responsible for its obligations, including payment.

If the supplier has taken over the equipment, it may take over the existing maintenance agreements from the customer.

Which of the parties has the better negotiating power to deal with the maintenance providers? It may be a customer who is a major organization with a number of associated companies, or an outsourcing supplier with many customers using the same equipment or software. The costs will be the customer's, whoever is the negotiator.

Where equipment is replaced by the supplier, it may be doing so as agent for the customer so that the equipment belongs to the customer, or in its own name, but for exclusive use by the customer in the services. It may be doing so in its own right, especially where the equipment is used for a number of the supplier's other customers too.

The extent of the customer's involvement in the purchasing decisions in respect of equipment exclusively for its use should be clarified. The customer may expect to be consulted on the specification and financing and to know about what is being proposed in advance, or it may be content to leave the buying decisions entirely to the supplier.

When the outsourcing contract comes to an end, there may need to be an agreed procedure for selling on to the customer any equipment purchased in the supplier's name for the customer's sole use on to the customer, ideally at a previously agreed price formula. The transfer of these assets at the expiry or termination of the contract may be a material factor in assessing whether the legislation on staff transfer, as discussed in the next chapter, will apply in respect of the staff concerned.

Human Resources

Requirements for the employees of both supplier and customer must be covered in the outsourcing contract. The customer must verify the experience and competence of the supplier's staff involved operationally. Reasonable restraints on one party's recruiting staff from the other may be stipulated, amongst other staff matters to be dealt with in the contract. But the major risk to cover contractually is that the customer's employees may be transferred to the supplier as part of the outsourcing process. They have particular legal rights in many outsourcing situations, whatever the size of the customer's, or indeed supplier's, organization. This is a fundamental concern for the outsourcing supplier. The customer also needs to be aware of the issues which should be covered in the contract. For this discussion the customer organization will be referred to as the 'transferor' of the staff and the outsourcing company will be the 'transferee'.

Supplier's staff

The quality and continuity of the supplier's staff who are to deliver the services will be of immense interest to the customer, who will have been assessing the supplier's personnel who have been put forward to respond to the invitation to tender, who have been making the presentations, giving assurances about what can be provided, and who are negotiating the contract.

In general the customer may need contractual assurances about the availability of sufficient suitably qualified and skilled staff, at the appropriate level for what is required, particularly if the charges for staff are directly levied on the customer, so that payment will be for a number of staff at each of a number of levels of experience. The customer may reserve the right to veto the appointment of any staff on reasonable grounds such as security if this is salient, and to exclude those who do not conform to agreed principles such as non-discrimination or compliance with staff regulations. In such cases, the customer may require the immediate replacement of any employee of the supplier who individually is found to be in persistent or material breach of the service obligations under the agreement, or in the case of reasonable suspicion of fraud, dishonesty or serious misconduct. This will be hard for the supplier to resist.

Some continuity in the supplier's staff will reasonably be anticipated by the customer, so that payment is genuinely for the provision of services and not for duplication of effort or training purposes by bringing in new personnel who have to learn the customer's ways of working. The customer does not want the supplier's staff to become experienced and knowledgeable in its applications and then to be moved elsewhere. Conversely, the supplier's staff will have a career structure, and will move from post to post for promotion or to gain different experience. For key personnel only, it may be feasible to negotiate a minimum period for which they should be carrying out the work for the customer, the giving of sufficient notice if it is intended to move them to different work, and the power to agree substitutes if changes are made. Nevertheless, there can be no absolute certainty about any particular individuals, who have their own careers to consider and may choose to resign and go elsewhere.

Each party may wish to have some say in the appointment or any replacement of the other party's senior representatives, as the people in these roles will work closely together and will be vital to the success of the outsourcing relationship. This is dealt with in Chapter 9. Tension may arise in the negotiations if the customer expects to be able to participate in the choice of successors to any staff of the supplier who leave, other than the personnel agreed as key to the outsourcing functions.

Restraints on recruitment

Staff working closely with staff of another employer may find that employer more attractive than their own. In a long term outsourcing contract or in selective outsourcing with no features of business transfer, either the customer or the supplier or both may be apprehensive about this. An employer may want to restrict recruitment of its employees by the company either for whom or by whom services are being provided, respectively.

If this is an issue, a provision in the contract will give some limited protection. Employers are not entitled to impose restraints on ex-employees merely to protect their own competitive position. Employees are free to choose for whom they would like to work, and cannot be prevented from responding to an open advertisement for employment as an independently considered career move. However, a carefully worded restraint clause will prevent active enticement by one party of the other's key personnel directly involved in the services being carried out under the contract for the duration of the contract. The safeguards in drafting an appropriate clause should include reasonable time limits (weeks or months, rather than years) and geographical restrictions. The individual circumstances of the employment situation will always affect what will be regarded as acceptable. The courts carefully scrutinise the extent of such restrictions in reviewing whether the actual wording used constituted what was necessary for an employer to protect its investment or whether it went beyond what was reasonable.

Other human resource considerations

The area of greatest legal risk in relation to staff which arises in outsourcing concerns the transfer of staff from the customer to the supplier.

The responsibility for such employment matters as work permits, legal and other costs, taxation, for the staff carrying out the outsourcing services, must unequivocally be the supplier's as the employer of the staff.

Concerns for the customer may arise over confidentiality, which should be covered by an express commitment by the supplier, as discussed in Chapter 11, and specifically in relation to TUPE, later in this chapter.

Points which should be covered in the contract for the benefit of both parties may arise in relation to human resources when the contract comes to an end. This is discussed in this chapter and in Chapter 12 which is about contract termination.

Transfer of the customer's employees

Not all arrangements are by any means a wholesale move to the outsourcing provider, involving full scale staff takeover together with acquisition of computer equipment and a licence or lease of premises. Yet with much less than this, there may be deemed to be an automatic transfer of the customer's employees to the supplier at law whether or not either party deliberately intends this to happen. This is because of the legislation applying to business transfers of various kinds, which may include outsourced service provision, and its interpretation in the courts. This leads to implications for potential liability by either party in respect of employees. Up-to-date specialized employment law advice should therefore always be taken, particularly as the rules and their application do change as a result of court decisions in individual cases.

Both the customer and the supplier should treat employment issues sensitively. It is not unknown for a potential outsourcing to be put at risk by current staff. The knowledge that outsourcing is going to take place creates great uncertainties for the customer's staff, who may be anxious about what is to happen to them and their jobs. As soon as staff learn that outsourcing is an option being considered, some of them may find other employment and resign rather than wait and see what will happen, fearful of suffering unwanted upheavals in their working lives. If key staff leave, it can become difficult for the customer to keep the IT systems running satisfactorily, making them less attractive for a supplier to take on.

Yet some staff may welcome the opportunity to move to a new employer with enhanced career prospects and increased variety of work, where IT is a core function of the business. The outsourcing may act as a catalyst to motivate them, with access to a wider range of computer career opportunities and broader training possibilities. An outsourcing supplier may have more of a vested interest than a user in keeping up with the latest technology and methodologies, and in educating employees to be flexible in acquiring new skills and responsibilities. The supplier may have been selected partly on the basis of its knowledge of the customer's industry sector. The adaptable employee who transfers with know-how gained from working in a specific kind of business will have useful expertise for the new employer and for a future career.

For those staff being transferred from the customer to the supplier's employment, the customer must take account of the intangible and not easily quantifiable risks of the loss of corporate experience, of a loss of understanding the political nuances of actions and decisions. This can make it difficult to envisage ever bringing the contract back in-house.

Initially the staff transferred will share some identity with the customer organization to which they used to belong. They will not need any training to understand the services being delivered and the context of those services. But their new career path will lie within the structure of the supplier's company, and their loyalties will change over time.

EC Directive and UK Regulations

The UK law which applies to the transfer of employees under outsourcing arrangements is the 'Transfer of Undertakings (Protection of Employment)' Regulations 2006'.[1] The regime is often known as 'TUPE', deriving from the initials of the principal words, familiarly pronounced 'Choopy'. They will be referred to in this chapter as the 'Regulations'. They replace previous Regulations and are based on European Union law, a Directive[2] referred to in this chapter as the 'Directive', which repealed and replaced earlier Directives, and applies throughout the European Union.

Purpose of the legislation

The purpose of the Directive, and therefore of the Regulations, is to safeguard employees' rights when a business is transferred to a new employer, or on a change in service provision where activities are outsourced, assigned to a new contractor or returned in-house from provision by an external contractor.

The Regulations require continuity of employment for employees within the scope of the outsourcing; the contracts of employment continue after the transfer, the new employer being substituted for the former employer. The contracts automatically transfer to the new employer. There is limited ability for any changes to be made, with or without the consent of the employees. Under this legislation it is not possible to avoid liability by dismissing employees before the transfer takes place.

Historically vendors (especially vendors of businesses in financial difficulties) used to be able to sell a business without its work force as a more attractive prospect for a purchaser. If the employer's identity changed, the employees' contracts of employment could be brought to an end. If a new employer retained the staff it would be in a strong position to set employment terms and conditions for exactly the same job which were inferior to those under which the employees had previously worked. The employees would also have lost the rights accrued as a result of length of service for continuity of employment in redundancy or dismissal situations.

The legislation was consequently introduced as a matter of public policy to protect employees when companies were restructured, or when there were mergers with other companies or acquisitions of the businesses in which the

---

1   Transfer of Undertakings (Protection of Employment) Regulations 2006 SI 2006/246.
2   Acquired Rights Amendment Directive 2001/23/EC.

employees worked. It came to be applied in the context of outsourcing, arguably by extension beyond the intended scope. The laws were not well drafted and there was much uncertainty in knowing how they would be interpreted in any individual case. The law developed through cases brought to court both in the UK and in Europe from the late 1970s and early 1980s onwards. In consequence, the Directive and the Regulations have sought to clarify the law.

Business transfers and changes of service provision

The Regulations apply to protect employees' rights on the 'transfer' of an 'undertaking' or business, or when there is a change in service provision. These circumstances are referred to as 'relevant transfers'. Some relevant transfers will be both a business transfer and a service provision change. There are particular rules in respect of insolvent businesses, which are not relevant for IT outsourcing service provision, and will not be discussed in this chapter.

For a business transfer, the transfer must be of an 'economic entity which retains its identity' after the transfer to a different employer. 'Entity' means an ascertainable group of employees carrying out the particular business activities, who will continue to do so after the transfer.

Where part of a business is being transferred, the Regulations will generally apply where that part is separately identifiable. It is immaterial if the part being transferred is incidental to the main business of the customer transferor. There does not have to be any transfer of goodwill, assets or specialist know-how.

The Regulations do not apply to transfers by share takeovers, since the identity of the employer itself does not change, even if the share ownership does. They generally do not apply to sales of assets in themselves, for example, sale of land or plant alone.

A change of service provision takes place when a 'grouping of employees' organized for the main purpose of providing services for their employer (the transferor), continue to carry out the services after there is a change to a new employer (the transferee). This definition includes outsourcing, assignment to a new contractor on subsequent re-tendering, and in-sourcing if the transferee takes the service back. 'Grouping' means that the same team of employees carry out the activities – although the 'team' may consist of no more than one employee. It excludes the situation where different people carry out the activities on an ad hoc basis, or tasks of a short duration, or the provision of services once for a specific purpose and a defined single event. It applies to services, not to the supply of goods.

The Regulations will also apply on the termination of the outsourcing contract, if the contractor loses the contract to a competitor or the services revert in-house, provided that there is a stable economic entity as described earlier, and the exclusions do not apply. The contracts of employment of the staff working within the area of the transfer will transfer from the supplier to the replacement supplier or back to the customer if the services are being taken back in-house.

Within the public sector, the conditions for business transfers or change of service provision under the Regulations may not be fulfilled. Transfers or reorganizations of administrative functions are not 'relevant transfers'. However, the Government's Code of Practice on Workforce Matters in Public Sector Service Contracts applies instead, operating in the Civil Service, local authorities, the National Health Service and maintained schools. The Code covers public sector service contracts, where staff transfer from a public sector organization to the service provider, or subsequently from the service provider to a new provider following contract re-tender.

What the Regulations say

- On the transfer of a business or on a change of service provision, the contracts of employment of employees engaged in the business immediately prior to the transfer are not terminated; instead, they *automatically* transfer on the same terms and conditions to the transferee of the undertaking as if originally made between the employee and the transferee.[3] Overseas employees may be included.

- Any dismissal connected with the transfer – whether occurring before or after the transfer – is *automatically* unfair, unless there is an 'economic, technical or organizational reason entailing changes in the work force'.[4] This means that an employee has the right not to be dismissed for any reason to do with the transfer.

- Collective rights are also *automatically* transferred. However, the transferee is obliged to recognise independent trade unions only if

3   Regulation 4.
4   Regulation 7.

the group being transferred has an identity which is distinct from the rest of the transferee's business. If this is not the case, there will no longer be trade union recognition.

In circumstances in which the Regulations apply, at the point of transfer the transferor's employees previously engaged in providing the services will immediately become employees of the transferee, on their then existing terms and conditions together with all of their accrued rights of continuous service – for example, redundancy rights, leave rights, etc. (together with accrued liabilities) – whether the transferee positively wants all the staff or not. This means that the staff will retain continuity of employment from the transferor. Any attempt to modify their terms and conditions will constitute grounds for a claim for constructive unfair dismissal (and will also be void). If employees' working conditions are changed for the worse following the transfer, such as a major relocation, they may have grounds to terminate their employment and claim unfair dismissal. The employees affected by the proposed outsourcing will therefore transfer unless they are retained in the transferor's organization.

Transfers, dismissals and employment claims

Dismissals related to the transfer will be automatically unfair unless the employer can show that they are for economic, technical or organizational reasons entailing changes in the work force. An economic reason must relate to the way the business is conducted. Changes to the work force by reason of changes in job functions or numbers of people involved or that the contract for service provision would be uneconomic to run, have been held to be valid reasons. These reasons would make the dismissal fair, provided that the test of reasonableness under unfair dismissal legislation succeeds.

A dismissal for a reason which is nothing to do with the transfer is potentially fair, if it meets the fairness tests in the unfair dismissal legislation.

If either the transferor or the transferee dismisses anyone who was engaged in the business before the time of the transfer, or shortly afterwards, where the main reason is the transfer, but not because of economic, technical or organizational grounds, then the transferee can be brought before an employment tribunal for the unfair dismissal of that employee – provided that the employee has been employed for at least one year and can show a significant change to his or her detriment. The dismissal will be automatically unfair. An award will be made against the transferee for payment to the ex-employee. Reinstatement or re-engagement are also remedies (and might then include a requirement for back pay).

Any dismissals which are seen to be the result of collusion between the transferor and transferee will be considered to be transfer-connected dismissals and will thus come under the legislation.

One case in which dismissals were held not to be related to the transfer concerned a situation in which the London Borough of Ealing Council contracted out its technical support work to Brown & Root Ealing Technical Services Limited. Two years later Brown & Root faced financial difficulties because the contract arrangements were underfunded. Ealing Council delayed in adjusting the payments until a dispute between the parties was resolved. Consequently Brown & Root tried to negotiate changes to the terms and conditions of employment of the transferred employees. Some accepted. Others were dismissed and offered new or amended terms of employment. A number of employees claimed that the dismissals were automatically unfair because the principal reason for them was the transfer or reasons connected with it.[5] They did not succeed. It was held that the reasons for the dismissals were the underfunding and the delay in amending the contract arrangements. These events had intervened between the transfer and the dismissals.

The transferor is still entitled to dismiss an employee on the grounds of actual misconduct in breach of the employment contract. Such a dismissal where the reason is unrelated to the transfer will be subject to the rules on unfair dismissal.

It would be difficult to argue that redundancies are being made for an economic, technical or organizational reason if services are being outsourced to a supplier, and the same work still continues, having become the supplier's responsibility. Under the legislation any former employees of the transferor laid off prior to contracting out because of the outsourcing, will have a claim against the transferee. Nevertheless, genuine redundancies effected in a workforce after transfer may be justifiable, as a potentially fair reason for dismissal. Ordinary unfair dismissal law applies; people must be selected fairly for redundancy, and proper redundancy procedures should be followed. An employee must have two years' employment service to benefit from statutory redundancy payments.

5 *Norris & Ors v Brown & Root Ealing Technical Services Ltd* [2002] All ER (D) 143.

Economic reasons may require such changes in the workforce. It is not always possible in all circumstances to safeguard the rights of workers. A transferee service provider might take the workforce and implement a redundancy programme if there were no longer any need for the work concerned because of 'some other substantial reason' for the dismissal, not simply the transfer of the business, provided that the redundancies were genuine and fair in themselves and complied with procedural requirements for consultation and selection. The employees concerned would be entitled to redundancy payments if they met the requirements of at least two years' employment service.

However, a transferee would normally be advised to delay making changes until well after the transfer period if possible, to avoid the risk of any dismissals or redundancies being considered to be transfer-connected. Cases have often arisen because, although a single redundancy or one unfair dismissal can be compensated, the principle may apply to many employees in a similar situation, all of whom would be entitled to compensation on the same grounds.

Other employment claims which could have been legitimately made by an employee against the transferor, such as for breach of contract or unlawful discrimination, could be made against the transferee, even if the claim was about events which happened before the transfer. The transferee would be liable under the employment contracts taken over, including, for example, any compensation – including sex discrimination compensation, where there is no set limit on the amount which can be awarded.

The effect of this is that the transferee outsourcing provider may not merely pick and choose those employees perceived to be of most use, and must ensure that suitable indemnities from the transferor are given in the contract.

Employees who consider that they have a case for breach of their employment rights may wish to make a claim to an employment tribunal. They may be advised by their trade union if they belong to one, or take professional legal advice. There are procedures which should be followed, and it is advisable for them to make contact first with the Advisory, Conciliation and Arbitration Service (ACAS).[6] The claim should be made within three months of the date on which the employment ended. There are some exceptions at the discretion of the employment tribunal, one of which is that it was 'not reasonably practicable' for the claim to be presented in time. It might not be reasonably practicable due to ignorance of a matter which is essential to the claim. For example, it has been held that an employee who found out three months after her redundancy that

---

6   htpp://www.acas.org.uk.

someone had replaced her could not reasonably have brought her complaint earlier.[7] The time limit might then be related to the date on which an employee, apparently made redundant, actually became aware that a transfer was taking place or had taken place, which might be longer than three months from the date of termination of employment. An employee who wishes to claim a redundancy payment should apply within six months of the dismissal.

Where there has not been a dismissal, and the employee has apparently openly accepted employment with the new employer by transfer, but there are discrepancies in wages or salary, a claim may be brought several months after transfer to recover difference in pay between the old and the new employment.

Where there is unfair dismissal, the employee may be reinstated or re-engaged or awarded compensation. Where the employee has suffered detriment, compensation may be payable according to what the tribunal considers to be just and equitable in the circumstances.

The claim may be made against the transferor, or the transferee, or both. If the claim is made only against one employer, then the other party may be joined to the case.

Pensions

The Regulations exclude occupational pension schemes from their main provisions insofar as they relate to old age benefits. Therefore any such obligations do not transfer. At the point of transfer, accrued rights are frozen. The employee will have the option of taking a deferred pension, or transferring funds into the transferee's scheme or into a personal pension fund

However, the law does require transferees to make pension provision for transferred staff,[8] and there are statements of practice and codes which apply to pensions in the public sector.[9] This essentially means that if the transferor provided a pension scheme, the transferee has to provide a certain minimum standard pension arrangement for employees who were eligible for, or were members of, the transferor's scheme, by means of an occupational pension

---

7   *Machine Tool Research Association v Simpson* [1988] IRLR 212.
8   Under the Pensions Act 2004, sections 257 and 258, and The Transfer of Employment (Pensions Protection) Regulations 2005 (SI 2005/649).
9   Cabinet Office Statement of Practice and Fair Deal for Staff Pensions; the Code of Practice on Workforce Matters in Local Government.

scheme (final salary scheme or money purchase scheme) or a stakeholder scheme.

Notification about employees transferring and data protection

The Regulations require the transferor to notify the new employer in advance of the transfer about the employees who will be transferring, with what is called 'employee liability information'.[10] The deadline for doing this is no later than fourteen days before the date of the transfer. The transferor must ensure that the information is kept up to date, and any changes also notified. It must include the identities of the employees, their ages, the information in their written statements of employment particulars, details of any disciplinary or grievance proceedings in the last two years, any legal action or potential litigation, and any relevant collective agreements. The sanction is that if this does not happen, the transferee can make a compensatory claim for each employee for whom the information was not provided or was defective, and there is a minimum award of £500 per employee (payable to the new employer). It is not possible to contract out of this obligation. Terms and conditions may go back for many years and may have themselves been inherited from a previous employer, not even necessarily through outsourcing but through acquisition or merger.

The requirement for employee liability information is in conflict with data protection legislation, because the employers will be disclosing their employees' personal data. However, guidance from the Information Commissioner's Office[11] confirms that this disclosure is permissible because it is 'required by law'. The disclosure must conform to general data protection principles so that the information should be accurate, up to date and secure, only transferred as necessary, and the transferee employer must use information only for the purposes for which it has been disclosed, that is for assessing potential liabilities or planning how the employees are to be integrated.

Following the transfer to the new employer, personnel records may be transferred for the purpose of the transfer and the business requirements. The transferee employer should review the information to check that it is all necessary to hold, and get rid of superfluous data. The transferor employer will need to keep employees' personal information for various reasons, for example in case of queries or liabilities.

---

10 Regulation 11.
11 Disclosure of employee information under TUPE available at http://www.ico.gov.uk.

The Information Commissioner may issue an Enforcement and Information Notice for failure to comply with the Data Protection Act in respect of employees' personal data, which could lead to criminal sanctions, or may impose a civil penalty for a serious data protection breach.

In practice therefore, staff must be trained in what they are entitled to do and how to do it properly under TUPE legislation and data protection legislation. A non-disclosure undertaking should be given by the potential supplier to use the information only for the purposes of TUPE. As soon as possible, employees should be informed that their information is to be transferred.

Varying employment terms

The Regulations cannot be disregarded, even by consent. The reasoning is that employees' rights arising out of transferred contracts of employment must be safeguarded by redressing the inherent imbalance of power in the employment relationship. It is not therefore legally permissible for an employee and the new employer to reach agreement that variations to the contract of employment will be acceptable following the transfer of the undertaking, simply because of the transfer. Even if there is some compensation for the variation, or the transferred employee positively gives consent, this agreement will not be enforceable.

Although such rights may not be waived under the legislation, an employee does have a fundamental legal right not to be compelled to work for an employer not of that employee's choice. However, the contract of employment of an employee who objects and refuses to transfer will be terminated, and the employee will then be left with no rights, losing any entitlement to redundancy or unfair dismissal. The exception to this is if the employee resigns because of justifiable fears that the terms and conditions imposed by the transferee will be worse, and would effectively amount to a fundamental breach of contract. The employee may then claim constructive dismissal against the transferor.

If the transfer results in a 'substantial change in working conditions to the material detriment of the employee' and the employee resigns in consequence, this will be taken as a 'deemed dismissal' by the transferor, with notice. The employee will not be able to claim notice pay, but will have all other rights.

Variations made for the sole reason of the transfer are unlawful. Changes to employment contracts in order to harmonize terms with those of existing employees of the transferee are therefore not permissible because the transfer would be the only reasons behind the change. This should be set in the context of employment contracts generally. An employer cannot unilaterally impose new terms and conditions without the employee's agreement. At some time it will become distant enough from the date of transfer for changes to be made to terms and conditions of employment that are not perceived to be made by the transferee solely on account of the transfer, but there is no generally understood time scale beyond which in practice the transferee can be confident of this.

Consultation

Where it is intended that employees will be transferred, meaningful consultations must be initiated as early as possible, either with any recognised trade union or, as an alternative, with employee representatives elected on an ad hoc basis or in advance, in respect of employees whom it is intended to transfer and also those who will stay behind.[12] The transferee will need to consult its own staff who may be affected by any measures taken in relation to the transfer.

Consultation will include information on the fact of the transfer, the reasons for it, and when it is to happen; the legal, social and economic implications; and the measures planned in relation to the employees. In the course of consultation, the employer must consider and reply to any representations made by employee representatives, with reasons if any of the representations are rejected.

Recognition of trade unions is not a legal requirement in the UK. Many customer organizations will have neither formal recognition agreements nor informal channels of consultation. In such cases, the transferor must consult with other appropriate representatives. These may have to be elected for this purpose, if none exist. There are rules for the election arrangements, and the elected representatives have rights to enable them to carry out their function of representation properly.

Both transferor and transferee are jointly and severally liable in the event of failure to provide information and to hold consultations with employee representatives. This could lead to a complaint being presented to an employment tribunal by the trade union concerned, employee representatives or affected employees. The deadline for bringing complaints is three months after the date on which the transfer was completed. An employment tribunal may award compensation payments of up to thirteen weeks' pay for each employee affected, which could include employees other than those directly concerned in the transfer.

---

12   Regulation 12.

Subsequent outsourcing

For outsourcing or return in-house to the customer at the conclusion of the outsourcing contract, the same rules apply. Relevant staff will transfer to the new supplier (or back in-house) from the original transferee on their existing terms and conditions. Continuity of employment, accrued rights and accrued liabilities transfer. The original transferee must consult and inform with staff, and provide employee liability information to the new employer.

To counter any potential problems, the original transferor customer might try to control the transferee's right to change the terms and conditions of employment of those employees who carry out the outsourcing work for the transferor, or any move to other work by those employees. The transferee is likely to regard this as an unreasonable fetter on its relationship with the employees.

What the Regulations mean in practice

The transferee takes over the liability for all statutory rights, claims and liabilities in respect of the contracts of employment of transferred staff, for example, health and safety disputes or liabilities in unfair dismissal and discrimination. Criminal liabilities and occupational pension benefits are exceptions to this rule. An employee may therefore make a claim against the transferee employer even if the breach of contract or discrimination for which the claim is being made took place before the transfer.

It would be sensible for the transferor customer to appoint someone very early in the process, to take overall responsibility for human resources, who can implement the general strategy and the procedures for keeping staff informed and involved, by complying with the legal requirements, and for working with trade unions if appropriate. Staff should be informed that information about their employment must be disclosed about staff to potential transferees, although this will be anonymised in the first instance, until it is known which employees will be transferring.

After the transfer, any claim for unfair dismissal may be brought against the transferee instead of the transferor. The costs of unfair dismissal compensation will therefore fall on the supplier. This aspect of the contract is essentially a matter of risk evaluation and assessment for the transferee, who must carry out a detailed due diligence on the employee situation, and, in determining the price, must build into the overall financial calculations an allowance for the potential financial liabilities, such as pre-existing employment liabilities, and include appropriate indemnities in the contract.

In any case in which the Regulations may apply, it is essential for both parties to take specialist up-to-date legal advice in respect of staff issues, and the earlier this is sought, the better. Apart from the practical decision of assigning the staff to the services to be provided, the transferee will take advice into account in order to price the contract to cover for maximum legal risk, and to require warranties and/or indemnities against any possible historic pre-transfer liabilities. The risks are not simply those of non-compliance but the costs of subsequently deciding to change the structure of the work force in a way which will be legal.

If the Regulations apply, the transferor will acquire all the customer's employees providing the services being outsourced. It is open for a transferor business which wishes to contract out part of its activities to offer alternative employment to those of its employees who would not wish to be transferred. It may wish to retain in-house expertise. It may transfer to another part of its business any key staff it does wish to retain before the negotiations get under way.

As a matter of commercial negotiation, the risks may be split between transferor and transferee.

Where there has not been a dismissal, and the employee has apparently openly accepted employment with the new employer by transfer, but there are discrepancies in wages or salary, a claim may be brought several months after transfer to recover difference in pay between the old and the new employment.

It is important for the transferor and transferee to agree on responsibility for each issue and each cost.

The contract

Provision for the transferee to acquire information about the employees must be made in negotiating the contract. A list of employees to whom the Regulations may apply will be agreed between the parties, for the contract. The employee information should be included in the relevant schedule or transfer agreement. The transferor should warrant in the contract that the information provided is accurate and complete. The transferor should also confirm that consultation took place properly and indemnify the transferee against any liability in this respect.

It is advisable to have comprehensive provisions about the ongoing notification of employee information throughout the provision of the services in the transfer agreement. This will assist when structuring any future transfers or service provision changes.

The parties should provide cross-indemnities to protect against liability for failure to consult employees about the outsourcing, and for pre- and post-transfer liabilities. The transferor should indemnify the transferee against any losses from pre-transfer breaches of contracts or of employment law in respect of the staff, for actions and omissions concerning employees prior to the transfer, in respect of claims by transferred employees arising from the outsourcing.

Thus the contract should entitle the transferor to be given information about the transferee's staff at the termination or expiry of the contract, in the same way as on entering into the outsourcing contract, as much as is necessary for the invitation to tender for submission of bids for the next outsourcing contract, in case the Regulations will apply to the transfer of staff to another different contractor. The transferee should warrant the accuracy of the information. The transferor and any successor contractor must be protected by indemnities from the transferee in relation to employment liabilities during the term of the outsourcing, and concerning the consultation process.

If the services are not brought back in-house at the conclusion of the outsourcing contract, the original customer transferor will seek indemnities which will benefit its new supplier outsourcing relationship, so that the new supplier can cost the services realistically.

The risk for the supplier would be to ignore the potential effect of the legislation on transfer of staff. This risk should be addressed in assessing the costs and pricing the outsourcing to allow for the risk and by including the appropriate provisions, warranties and indemnities in the contract.

The customer should limit its own risks by offering indemnities only to the extent that they are reasonable.

One reported anecdote shows the importance of analysing what the objectives of outsourcing are intended to be. One industrial equipment manufacturer outsourced because it was felt that the IT staff did not have the technical skills necessary to implement a new computer architecture. Yet in the outsourcing those same IT staff were transferred to become employees of the supplier. The manufacturer had not solved the underlying problem and the whole arrangement failed. The customer's unqualified staff became the supplier's unqualified staff.[13]

---

13 Willcocks and Fitzgerald, 1994, *A Business Guide to Outsourcing IT*, Business Intelligence Limited.

Software

Rights of ownership and use of the intangible assets involved in the IT services are valuable, yet vulnerable to being overlooked in the outsourcing contract. The major concern will normally be for software, and this is the main focus of this chapter. A section later on discusses the treatment of databases, which should also be considered in this context.

The origins of the various software used by the customer's IT department for the purpose of running its systems are likely to vary. The software may have been designed and coded by the customer's staff. It may have been written partly by employees and partly by freelance contractors, or it may have been commissioned externally. It may have been acquired from, or licensed by, a third party owner or distributor of the software. It may be a simple packaged product supplied in volume to numbers of users, or it may be highly customised or uniquely designed for the customer's business requirements. An important part of the process of negotiating the contract is to ensure that the software not owned by the supplier or transferred to it is correctly licensed for the supplier's use, and the ownership defined. The ways of dealing with software to be used in the future must also be considered. Before an IT outsourcing contract is finalised, the licensing or ownership arrangements for all the different software must be agreed.

Once the outsourcing is in operation, the supplier will be using the software in order to operate systems, process data and generate results. The supplier must have proper authorizations granted by the different owners of the software in order to have the rights to run the various software packages and systems legitimately. Authorization is normally demonstrated by means of licences which grant permission for use of the software under specified circumstances and impose stipulations to circumscribe that use.

The first part of this chapter outlines the reasoning behind the contractual provisions which should be made in respect of the software. An explanation is given of what is meant by ownership rights in software, so far as this is relevant for the purposes of the outsourcing contract. It describes what entitlements are conferred on the owners of the rights, and how they come into effect; how use of software is validly permitted; and the assurances which will normally be given by the software owner to the user.

Next, the different arrangements are considered which should be made for software owned by third parties; any software owned by the supplier which the supplier will be using for the benefit of the customer; any software developed in the course of outsourcing; and finally any software belonging to the customer itself.

The ownership of the software carries implications for the ways the rights to use the software are obtained. Software in use in the customer's organization may belong to the customer itself, having been developed in-house, or because the customer has acquired the rights of ownership by assignment, perhaps having negotiated the rights for software which was specially commissioned. However, there will typically be many different kinds of software needed for running the customer's IT operation, which are not owned by the customer. This software will be in use under licences granted to the customer by third parties who either own the software themselves, or who have themselves been authorized by the software owner to grant licences.

In IT outsourcing, the supplier must have the right to run all the software, whether at the existing site or at a new site. For third party software, the supplier as user must be licensed by the third party software owner. It must also be clearly entitled to run software owned by the customer.

In general, the outsourcing supplier will be taking over responsibility for the software. It will be paying licence fees and maintenance and support charges to third party owners or other licensors. It will be implementing the upgrades and new versions. The costs to the supplier of doing this, and the fees themselves, must be factored into the overall charges or identified as separate chargeable items. The customer should seek indemnities from the supplier against software misuse, whether by the supplier itself or by a third party through the supplier's negligence or lack of security.

Finally, the contract should enable the customer to be able to use the software following termination of the arrangements. This is particularly important for software used in the provision of the services which is owned by the supplier.

What are 'rights' in software?

Those who own property of any kind have legal rights to enable them to protect their ownership. Property which cannot be seen or touched, and which comes into existence through some kind of creative effort is defined as 'intellectual' property. Software is one example of this, protected under UK law by means of the specific intellectual property right of copyright, which also applies to graphics, reports, manuals and other business or commercial documents, amongst other works. Copyright is a right derived from legislation, which is applicable within a legal jurisdiction. Thus in the UK it is a right created by Acts of Parliament and statutory instruments.[1] Other countries, in Europe, the USA or anywhere else, will have different ways of defining copyright under their laws and protecting software as property. Copyright is the most usual means, but the features and applicability of copyright differ from territory to territory. There are international treaties where agreement has been reached over particular aspects, in order to facilitate trade, and the specific aspects agreed will be carried into the copyright laws in force in the signatory countries. Similarly there are EU Directives relating to copyright, which each member state, including the UK, implements through its national laws.

This chapter is about software which is protected by copyright. Some software is patentable in the US and elsewhere. Under UK law,[2] software 'as such' and business methods inventions cannot be patented, although software which produces a technical effect may be patented.

Software which is business-specific or otherwise sensitive or which belongs in a category of 'trade secrets' may also need to be legally protected through confidentiality agreements – as may sensitive or secret information.

Entitlement to copyright is limited in time, to 70 years following the death of the author. This is clearly an unimportant limit at present as far as software is concerned.

Copyright protects 'original' work which has been recorded in some medium – visual or electronic. This does not mean for software that the coding needs to be especially innovative. It means that some individual contribution and effort has gone into producing it.

---

1   Principally the Copyright Designs and Patents Act 1988.
2   Patents Act 1977.

Copyright is a property right, potentially with economic benefits, arising automatically without any formalities such as registration. It is the exclusive right of the owner to copy, to issue copies or to adapt the copyright work, and consequently to stop others from copying. 'Copying' means reproduction in any material form. Running off a copy of the software on disc or storing the software electronically, constitutes copying just as much as photocopying or copying lines of code by hand. 'Adapting' includes modifying or translating the software, so that it may not be converted into another computer language or code without the software owner's permission.

It is not possible to use software without copying it, electronically or in hard copy, and so there is no accidental way of acquiring the right to use it.

As an economic right, copyright is therefore a means for software publishers and value added resellers to gain financially by making profits through licensing the software in order to recoup the investment which they have made in developing it. Licensing may also – or sometimes alternatively – be the basis for controlling use of the software as discussed below.

There is a problem in practice in interpreting the level at which the law operates in relation to copyright works, which leads to uncertainties. The copyright in a novel consists of the text of the novel, which may not be legitimately copied, translated or adapted without permission. It also prevents the structure of the unfolding of the story-line being copied, even if the words used were entirely different. But the plot itself at its most basic level is not protectable. At the other extreme, if there is only one way in which an idea may be expressed, such as a mathematical formula, copyright may not be successfully claimed for it. For software, similar functions may be performed by quite separate programs, where the respective programmers have each used completely different coding. It may nevertheless be claimed that the program written later is an infringement of the first, and that the structure and functions have been copied. This is known as the 'idea/expression' dichotomy, or 'look and feel'. If an allegation of copyright infringement is made about a piece of software which is not a straight copy, expert evidence, necessary for all copyright infringement proceedings if copying is not admitted, will be required to determine whether, on the balance of probabilities, copying has in fact taken place. However, it is very difficult to succeed in the UK for copyright infringement based on 'look and feel' – although each case will be judged on its particular facts.

The work preparatory to software publication – the flowcharts, user requirements, design specifications, program specifications – will also be subject to copyright.

The value in intellectual property rights is difficult to assess, and the book value may be much less than the value representing the investment made in its development and its market value relating to its scarcity, originality and functionality.

Who owns rights in software?

The first owner of copyright in software is its author, unless the author is an employee and wrote the software in the course of his or her work, when the author's employer will be the first owner. Note that a self-employed contractor or a consultant from an external agency or a freelance programmer, in providing services to an organization, is not an employee of that organization. They will therefore retain copyright in the work they do if there is no agreement otherwise. Although there will be an implied right for that organization to use the software for which it has paid, neither the commission itself nor payment for the work entitles that organization to ownership of the software.

If more than one programmer has contributed to the software development or if members of a team have collaborated in writing the programs, and the contributions are not distinct, there will be joint ownership. A system which consists of a collection or combination of individual programs and modules may belong to more than one copyright owner, and the combination or collection may itself be separately subject to copyright.

Where a number of freelance programmers are working on constituent parts of commissioned software, they may not individually be able to make any practical use of their own coding. However, their client who commissioned them, may wish to enhance or update the software at a later date, or to market it commercially. Ownership of the resulting software will be much more useful to the client in these circumstances than to the contractors, if the design and coding is unique to the software concerned.

Copyright can be transferred to another party by means of a formal agreement assigning the rights to the new owner. The contract for a contractor's services may therefore include assignment of the software which the contractor has been retained to write as part of the services being provided. Individual consultants or contractors will hold copyright in the work they produce if this assignment provision is not part of their contractual terms. In any event, they should not automatically sign their rights away if they are not providing exclusive services, or if the client is not going to gain any practical advantage from them doing so. If the contractors have particular routines or modules which they use again and again, they should certainly hold on to copyright.

Permission to use the software

Commercial software developers, publishers and distributors will not rely on basic legal copyright alone in marketing and supplying software. They will expect their customers and end users to enter into contractual arrangements for use of the software by means of software licence agreements. A licence will give the owner the opportunity to impose conditions in an effort to control and restrict authorized use of its asset. For example, the software will be limited to use only on a designated computer at a particular location or an identified business environment; for a specific number of concurrent end users. It must not be copied except under the conditions permitted in the licence; it must be kept confidential; and it must not be accessed by anyone other than the licensee. To a large extent, the licence fee will be related to these restrictions, to enable the licensor to charge additionally for an increase in the number of concurrent users, or extension to further sites, or as a result of a machine upgrade. Alternatively open source licensing permits studying, modification and redistribution of source code without the licensor directly profiting from these activities.

Whatever the licence states, a licensee has the right to make a copy for back-up purposes, and in certain limited circumstances a licensee would have a right to decompile the software. This latter right is exercisable only as necessary in order to obtain information required to create another independent program which needs to operate in conjunction with the software from which the decompilation is being carried out. The intention of this right, which resulted from European Community legislation with the purpose of enhancing free trade and competition, is to enable new interoperable (but not substitute) software to be created without permitting third party proprietary information to be misused in creating competing products.[3]

To relate the general principles of software copyright to outsourcing, the customer would normally be breaching the terms of its software licence

---

3   Directive on the Legal Protection of Computer Programs ('Software Directive') 91/250 EEC OJ 1991 L122/42 implemented – the UK by the Copyright (Computer Programs) Regulations; SI 1992/3233.

agreement if the outsourcing supplier was able to access the software without proper authorization.

The outsourcing supplier would be liable itself for unauthorized access. This will be the case if the customer continues to take the licence in its own name and pay for it, but the software is being accessed and used by the supplier under an outsourcing arrangement, without the licensor's knowledge and consent.

Existing licences to the customer from third party software suppliers will normally not extend automatically to outsourcing arrangements, but it is becoming more common to find that they are drafted widely enough to cover use for outsourcing, or they may have been modified during negotiations if the licensee was aware that outsourcing might be a future option for its organization. A software licensor may legitimately object to the licence terms being varied for outsourcing purposes. There are two principal reasons which could lie behind an objection. The first is that the outsourcing supplier may be a competitor of the licensor. Both of them may be in the same outsourcing market. In this situation the licensor would seek to create conditions to deter the outsourcing supplier from abusing its access to the software.

The other reason is for the licensor to protect its investment in developing the software. The licensor will normally permit the outsourcing supplier to run the software provided that the licence fee is increased to cover this use.

Without the licensing permissions in place, a customer would risk legal action being taken against it by the rightful owner for damages for breach of its current licensing conditions. The outsourcing supplier would risk criminal liability for using software without proper authorization.

Intellectual property rights indemnity

A professionally drawn software licence will normally include an indemnity from the owner of the software to cover the possibility of any third party claim of infringement being made against the licensee legitimately using the software under the terms of the licence. An example where the situation might arise is where software developed by the customer, using its own staff and contractors, is licensed by the customer to the supplier to run for outsourcing purposes. A third party contractor who had worked for the customer might have written a significant part of the software without assigning copyright to the customer at the time of carrying out the programming services. The contractor discovers that the software is valuable and being used successfully, and makes an allegation of infringement, asserting authorship. Going back to the definition of copyright, the claim would not be made out of possessiveness. It would be made because the claimant believed that there was an entitlement to a share in the economic value being derived from the software.

If there were to be a valid claim, an injunction might theoretically be obtained to inhibit future use of the software by the supplier, or the supplier might be liable in damages or for payment of royalties. It could be expensive for the supplier to counter the claim, in terms both of effort and of legal costs. After all, the supplier would be an innocent party in the situation, using the software only because of the customer's outsourcing requirements. The customer will therefore recognise its responsibilities by means of a limited indemnity in licensing the software.

An intellectual property rights indemnity in a software licence normally limits the licensor's liability to the licensee, and is subject to some control by the licensor over the claim being made; it is in the licensor's interest to take over the defence since the subject matter of the claim is an asset belonging to the licensor. Similarly, the indemnity which the supplier should expect the customer to provide in respect of its own software will not necessarily be so extensive. It will indemnify the supplier against any expense, loss or damage as a result of any claim that the supplier's use of the customer's software under the outsourcing contract infringes the intellectual property rights of a third party.

Administrative exercise

The review of all the licences for third party software comprised in the systems being outsourced normally involves substantial effort, to establish whether assignment or novation of the licence to the outsourcer is required, or whether the licence already allows for outsourcing. The earlier in the contractual process that the software negotiations with licensors are initiated, the better. Investigating the licence terms, drafting assignments and agreements, and negotiating the transfers with third party licensors, will probably involve far more time and effort than most customers anticipate. It will be a large part of the 'due diligence' exercise discussed in Chapter 1.

It is rare for all the customer's current software licences to be systematically gathered together in one place. Occasionally licences are missing. It is still relatively unusual to find a compliance system already established for the licence requirements: the number of copies allowed to be made, authorized access, confidentiality, and other conditions laid down by the licensor.

Employees may be unaware of the obligations set out in the software licences. They may not appreciate what the licence conditions state. The owner of the software may be unknown to them. This is the time to find out.

As part of this exercise, the software support and maintenance contracts should also be assembled and reviewed, ready for discussions with the licensor and supplier.

There is an ISO sandard for software asset management, which may be considered for use during the outsourcing: ISO/IEC 19770-1:2006 IT – Software Asset Management Part 1. It helps companies oversee and control software assets. It gives guidance on developing a software inventory, assessing suppliers' service level agreements and managing the assets throughout their lifecycle.

Third party software licences and support

A customer may use software continuously or regularly, yet this does not mean that it will have the right to deal with this software as it chooses.

Licences to the customer for bought-in software or for software developed and customized for it by a third party will contain a number of restrictions on use by the customer, as discussed earlier. Use will normally be confined to that customer – which would not necessarily extend to the customer's subsidiaries or associated companies – and the licence will normally prohibit any other party from using the software. This enables the licensor to retain control over the software comprising its intellectual property, and avoid the risk of it passing to a competitor.

The choice for the licensor is to transfer the licence to the outsourcing supplier or to extend the rights in the original licence to the outsourcing supplier. Use of the software may be unchanged, or there may be a wider or different use of the software, on account of the outsourcing.

Some licensors see outsourcing as a chance to increase their revenues, and will take the opportunity of charging relatively high fees for the assignment or transfer of licences to the outsourcing supplier. They may do so even where the software will in fact be running on the same machine, in the same building, linked with the same systems as before, and operated by the same staff. The terms of their licences with the customer may well cover their rights to do so. The software support costs may also be affected.

Nevertheless, the licensors of this software must be informed of the imminent outsourcing situation, for the supplier to acquire the appropriate permissions to run the software legitimately.

If the charges being imposed appear to be excessive, the customer must consider its options. It is strongly advisable to sort matters out at this stage, although it can take much longer to do so to everyone's satisfaction than may originally have been foreseen. The permissions should ideally all be in place at the point at which the outsourcing contract is signed, or at the latest the time when the contract comes into effect, if this is different. If they are ignored, the risk is that the licensor will take legal action against the customer for the extra payment, or even in order to discontinue the use of the software by the customer or the outsourcing supplier – or to take court proceedings for infringement of copyright, as the use would be beyond what was permitted in the original licence to the customer. There have been a number of cases in the UK in which the software owner has taken legal proceedings against the outsourcing supplier for copyright infringement, but they have been settled before a court hearing.

The customer must decide whether the software is really critical to its business. In the short term, it is almost inevitable that there will be no realistic alternative way of managing the business requirement.

From the customer's perspective, it may apparently be helpful if the outsourcing supplier can take on the responsibility for negotiating with third party software owners. The supplier may be experienced in doing this as a matter of course in setting up outsourcing arrangements, and know how best to approach the task. However, the costs will be passed on to the customer, and may be higher than the customer would have been able to negotiate for itself.

Sometimes the outsourcing supplier has its own licences for this purpose if other customers are using the same software. The supplier will already have dealt with the licensor in its right to use the software for numbers of customers. The licensing fees, perhaps at specially negotiated rates, can be spread over the customer base.

If the software owner creates difficulties by making exorbitant demands over important software, competition issues may be raised.

UK competition law is modelled on the European Union competition regime, with regard to trading within the UK.[4] Under Article 82 of the Treaty of Rome, European Union law directly applicable within the UK, a company with a dominant position in its market is not permitted to abuse that position in a way which weakens competition if trade between member states would be adversely affected.[5] The dominance is of the particular market sector in which the company operates, such as the supply of specialised software or services, and is assessed by market share or by the company's ability to behave independently of its competitors in stopping effective competition. A dominant company is able to distort competition in its market, for example by setting unfairly high prices or predatory low prices, or imposing different prices for the same product in different regions. Thus the dominant company is not entitled to take advantage of its market position, such as through discriminatory practices or unfair pricing – or refusal to license at a reasonable fee.

The Office of Fair Trading is responsible for applying and enforcing competition law in the UK, and has wide powers of investigation and enforcement.

From a practical point of view, valuable attention may be diverted from the time-consuming process of negotiating the outsourcing contract by having to take resources and effort to deal with the software vendor, with the concomitant risks of confrontation and costs. However, awareness of the competition angle may be a useful point to discuss in any negotiations with large software vendors who appear to be recalcitrant, if there is no substitute for using their software.

For third party software, the ideal time for the issues to be addressed is long before the outsourcing negotiations are in hand. If outsourcing is known to be a possible future option for the IT department, the matter should be raised at the point of negotiating licence terms and conditions for the procurement of new bought-in or specially commissioned software. This is the moment when the position of the customer will be at its strongest – when it has a choice of whether to take the software or to find an alternative.

As part of the original terms of supply of the software to the customer the licence may have been expressly extended, to allow for a future outsourcing situation, to preclude the need for any further negotiation between the licensor and the customer.

---

4   Competition Act 1998, Enterprise Act 2002.
5   EC Treaty Article 82 and Regulation 1/2003[2003] OJ L1/1.

The supplier's own software

Third party software may include the supplier's own proprietary software, which the supplier uses in providing or managing the outsourcing services. If the software becomes indispensable, there is a risk of reliance on it which could rebound to the detriment of the customer at the expiry or termination of the contract. The software should be licensed to the customer, ideally in terms permitting its use beyond any possible termination of the supplier's services, and potentially to license a future service provider. The customer should try to negotiate ongoing rights to use the source code of the software or for the source code to be held independently by an escrow agent, as discussed later. It would then be available to the customer in the event of failure of the supplier's business or if the supplier defaulted in providing the services.

The customer's software licences

For software owned by the customer, it will be a simple matter for the supplier to be expressly permitted to run the systems using that software by the grant of a licence within the outsourcing contract itself. If the customer has developed its own software using in-house staff, or if it has acquired rights of ownership to bought-in software by assignment, or if the software has been developed by external contractors for the customer under contracts for services assigning the contractors' rights in the software to the customer, there will not be any problem for the supplier in using that software in the outsourcing. No third party will be involved.

The customer must formally grant a licence to the supplier, as a provision in the agreement, stating that the supplier is licensed to use the customer's software for the purposes of providing the outsourcing services. The minimum obligations for the supplier are to agree by means of formal wording as part of this clause not to use the software for any other purpose, not to disclose it other than for the performance of the services, and to acknowledge its confidentiality. The customer may also require assignment to it of copyright of any modifications and enhancements made to the software by the supplier as part of the services. It would also be normal for the customer to provide the supplier with an intellectual property rights indemnity, as discussed earlier in this chapter.

A licence is preferable to a once-for-all assignment of the software by the customer to the supplier. Strategically it is in the customer's interests to retain ownership of its key systems and applications. In principle these have an asset value to the customer's company, and the supplier does not need absolute ownership – it will not be intending to exploit the software commercially. Mainly the software rights should be retained because the customer should always bear in mind in negotiating the outsourcing contract that there is the future possibility of the arrangement with the supplier coming to an end. If so the customer will still need to use its software. There is no need to hand over ownership of its software assets to the supplier.

Software developed in the course of outsourcing

The contract should be clear about ownership of new software, and enhancements to existing software developed by the supplier during the outsourcing process. The customer would normally expect to acquire ownership of additions, enhancements and modifications to its own software, and to ensure that there is comprehensive documentation by the supplier as they are implemented. If the outsourcing contract should be terminated, the customer will still use the software, and the additions and enhancements will not benefit the supplier.

Change of software during the contract term can be one of the most difficult areas in practice. For example, a supplier may choose to abandon the customer's proprietary software and substitute third party software, the justification being on grounds of efficiency. Does the customer have any say in this decision? What rights in the new software to take effect at the end of the contract term can be negotiated on behalf of the customer?

Documentation

Systems and procedures manuals and other documentation should not be ignored in the consideration of copyright. The same principles will apply although they will be simpler in practice, and negotiation will normally be less fraught. End users may need to use a number of user manuals. Customers should be expressly entitled in the contract to use the supplier's documentation.

'Escrow' (source code deposit)

For some systems, neither the supplier nor the customer will have access to source code.

Licences for third party software in a typical installation will be for the software in object code or interpreted format, which will be satisfactory in the ordinary course of events for run-time operation. Source code is the human-readable format, which theoretically enables an experienced programmer with expertise in the language in which the code is written to understand the structure of the program and the way in which it works after compilation or interpretation to achieve its application objective.

Thus for software which needs modification and enhancements from time to time, or which interfaces with other software which may be upgraded, access to source code is essential. However, this access would not inevitably be required by the customer. Provided that the licensor of the software or the third party maintainer has that access, whether by ownership or by source licence, it will be of no concern in normal circumstances to the customer in being itself prevented from holding a source licence. Apart from open source software, the owner will be seeking to protect its assets by keeping the source code to itself, providing support and upgrades as necessary from time to time.

Escrow agreements are a means of guarding against the consequences of the insolvency of the software owner, when support provision would cease. They may be negotiated with the software owner in circumstances where neither the supplier nor the customer has access to source code. A copy of the source code will be deposited with a neutral third party custodian for release only in certain situations prescribed in an escrow agreement between the software owner and third party custodian, to which the customer or licensee would also be a party. The normal situation for release would be the insolvency of the third party software supplier – not unusual in the volatile IT industry. If this happens, commitment made in advance by the software supplier to its customer by means of this separate escrow agreement to make a copy of the source code available would be enforceable against a liquidator, who would have taken over the assets of the software supplier company, including the asset of the software source.

The insolvency will therefore be an event which triggers the release of a copy of the software source by the third party custodian to the customer, to enable support and enhancements to continue to be provided until a purchaser is found for the software assets of the liquidated software company. Finding the appropriate programming knowledge and experience in understanding the source (in the state in which it has been deposited) to amend it may be more of a wistful hope than achievable in practice. Nevertheless this is the way in which source code deposit or 'escrow' has developed in the software industry.

The wording of existing escrow agreements relating to the software should be reviewed, to ensure that the benefit would continue to be available for the outsourcing supplier. Escrow arrangements must be considered for new software licensed during the outsourcing to permit access in the event of insolvency, and possibly in the event of failure by the software owner to maintain it. Suitable provision should be set out in the contract for this.

The supplier should also agree to put source code of its proprietary software used in the outsourcing into escrow, to guard against its own insolvency – when there would be other pressing concerns for the customer – or for passing the source to the customer on expiry or termination of the contract.

Databases

Collections of information are increasingly important – including websites. Within the European Union, a right known as the 'database right' prevents unfair extraction or re-utilization of the contents of a database.[6] 'Database' in this context means a collection of independent works, data or other material which are arranged systematically or methodically, and are individually accessed by electronic or other means. The right has been introduced for databases where there has been substantial investment in obtaining, verifying or presenting the contents, and the maker belongs within the European Economic Area.[7] It is not a comprehensive right which applies to all databases.

If the selection and arrangement of the EU databases are the result of their authors' own 'intellectual creation', they will be protected by copyright. That right prevents any unauthorized copying, adaptations or dealings in the database, in the same way as for software.

It is likely (although not inevitably so) that it will be less complicated to deal with databases than with software in an outsourcing situation. But the procedure of ensuring that the supplier has the right to deal with any database which is being used within the outsourcing, will be the same as for software. A licence from the rightholder, whether the customer or a third party, must be obtained.

The right lasts for fifteen years, following 'completion' of the database. Many electronic databases are the subject of constant small changes and updating

---

6   EU Database Directive 96/9 (OJ 1996 L77/20); Copyright and Rights in Databases Regulations 1997, SI 1997/3032.

7   This comprises EU member states + Norway, Iceland and Liechtenstein.

within their structure and main contents format, often from minute to minute. Such databases will never be 'completed' – the term will run continuously.

Procedure

Software licensing must be addressed early on in the outsourcing contract. Information needs to be collated by the customer for the supplier about the current owners of its software, and about the terms and conditions on which the software is licensed, followed by renegotiation, assignment or novation of some of the software. This can be a lengthy procedure.

Software licences affect the outsourcing costs as software publishers take the opportunity to charge for assigning their licences. Arrangements must be clarified for third party software, the supplier's software, the customer's software, and software developed, enhanced or modified during the term of the outsourcing.

The supplier may also need the right to use databases in the outsourcing, and this is most efficiently considered at the same time as the rights to use software.

Costs and Charges

Cost reduction should never be the sole criterion in the selection of an outsourcing supplier, but costs will always be one of the drivers in the customer's move towards outsourcing, whether or not savings over present IT costs are the customer's prime objective. IT expenditure which is foreseeable and manageable may be an additional or alternative target to be achieved, often explicitly. Whatever the reasoning, the customer will be intending to get value for money. In principle the costs should become more transparent and therefore more controllable.

Outsourcing experience varies as to whether customers get the expected financial benefits or lose out. Whether the charges made over the life of the contract are as predicted, and whether savings are achieved, will be affected by the way the contract is negotiated and finally worded, and the extent of changes to the services during the life of the contract.

Any invitation to tender or other opening request to an outsourcing supplier will always ask for proposals on charging. The different bids put forward will be considered and compared at an early stage in the selection process. Yet because of the details involved and the links with other parts of the contract such as its duration and the service levels, the detailed charging arrangements may become one of the last matters on which agreement is reached.

According to the extent and kinds of services to be provided, the negotiation processes may be convoluted and precision of expression in the contract hard to attain. A single contract may include a combination of charging methods, for different features of the services, drawn from a variety of pricing structures and costing mechanisms.

The charges may range from a global fixed price for the whole contract at one extreme through daily rates and direct costs, to intricate formulae for individual calculations at the other end of the scale. Components of the charges, such as staff or contractors' costs, data volumes and equipment rental, may be separately identified and itemised.

Allowance should be made for adjusting the charges during the life of the contract, to accommodate variations to the services, or to enable the supplier to cover its own rising costs. An opportunity for re-negotiation may be required by the customer where economies are anticipated over time by the supplier's efficiency or the introduction of more effective technological applications, or where the contract is for a lengthy fixed term.

The main body of the contract will set out the general obligation for the customer to pay the supplier the charges for the services and the payment terms which apply, with reference to a separate schedule or appendix where the details of the charges will be given. This is especially convenient where there are complicated, numerous or lengthy formulae or calculations. It also enables the schedules to be updated when the charges are varied.

Commercial evaluation

The customer's internal IT department costs are often treated as an overhead. Costs associated with IT may include those for the resources – the personnel and the management of the staff; office accommodation; computer hardware and networks; software licences; project development and implementation; and the recurring costs of maintenance and support.

In evaluating outsourcing charges, the customer should ideally be making direct comparisons with its own current budget. The projected costs of outsourcing can be compared over the years of the proposed contract term with the projected costs of retaining the service in-house. This must be done realistically, to take account of any changes which may arise from falling technology costs, as well as from requirements for new developments and more sophisticated systems. In practice, many customers do not have enough information to enable them to make an informed estimate of any potential savings.

In whatever way the charges are assessed, a familiar argument is that an individual customer is not going to be able to make the sorts of savings that one supplier acting for a number of customers can effect through economies of scale. The optimistic supplier's argument is that there are bound to be savings in all areas: hardware, software licences, site costs, staff and their expertise, help desk, back up and recovery, and other security matters. Some suppliers are undoubtedly going to be more cost-effective than the customer's previous internally organized management services department, either generally in providing information systems or running IT operations, or specifically in providing a particular service. One central help desk for a particular system platform may service end users from a number of different customer companies. The same hardware may be used efficiently for a range of customers, and there may be gains from price-performance technology improvements. The supplier may have negotiated a single licence with standard software suppliers. A number of customers' requirements may be able to be covered by a small number of technically experienced staff. The supplier's services may be able to be standardized, and thereby savings in overheads may be achieved. The supplier may be in a position to cut costs safely in ways which were politically unacceptable for an in-house service to effect.

The supplier will claim business experience in its customers' industries and that it is continuously keeping up to date technologically. The argument is that this must be to the benefit of its customers.

It depends to some extent on the nature of the outsourcing. Economies of scale are more easily demonstrable on stable mainframe and operations outsourcing, less obvious on systems development.

The converse argument is that any such economies can also be achieved by an efficient in-house department, which does not have substantial promotional costs, and which is not having to make a profit in its operation. In outsourcing the customer has to allow for the costs of new activities arising from management of an external function: management reviews of performance, audits and control of variations. A large customer organization whose operations are extensive, whose name is well known and who has a number of subsidiary or associated companies, may have negotiated its own discounts for the supply of technology or licence fees, which it may be reluctant to forego for an outsourcing arrangement. Licence transfer fees can be costly, and the supplier may gain little benefit for the customer by its own site licence.

If the outsourcing costs appear to be favourable, the customer may have to assess whether there are ways in which it could itself make equivalent savings in-house over a period of time. Where the outsourcing costs do not seem to be attractive, other factors may be brought into the equation. In deciding whether the supplier can provide the services more cheaply than the current in-house facility or whether the in-house department is more cost-effective, the implications of what the suppliers are offering must be reviewed.

Capital or revenue

The customer's financial motives may go further than a cost-cutting rationale or seeking predictability of costs. In some cases outsourcing will enable capital to be removed from a company's balance sheet, with the immediate strategic advantage of converting a fixed cost capital basis for IT activities to the variable costs of revenue-based IT services.

The customer is transforming fixed data processing assets into variable costs and will no longer have to find the capital to finance new technology or to make large scale future investment in IT.

When the supplier acquires equipment and staff from the customer, this may release capital and other financial resources. The main IT costs are for staff, and the most palpable way for the customer to make savings will be through the transfer of its IT staff to the supplier. At one fell swoop this will reduce the customer's overall IT costs, and aid its ongoing training and recruitment budget. The supplier may be able to make efficient use of the staff it acquires by using them for its services for the customer or elsewhere within its organization. The employment and career path of the transferred personnel will no longer be determined by the customer's IT requirements.

A computer may be purchased for cash by the customer, or may be obtained on a financial lease. In this latter case a liability in respect of that lease will be created on the balance sheet for the future cash requirements associated with the lease. Either way, the effect is to increase the gearing, that is the ratio of the amount of the company's capital in the form of debt to the amount in the form of shareholders' equity. Given that the computer – and linked equipment – is depreciating (otherwise the advantage gained will be only short-term) it can be sold to the supplier as part of the outsourcing arrangements, and the debt represented by it on the balance sheet will be removed. This will assist in reducing the customer's gearing. Money tied up on the balance sheet on non-financial assets, such as cars, property and computers, can be more valuable if released for core activities of an organization. It will also be a factor in the outsourcing evaluation by a company with too much debt.

As part of the overall balancing of the transaction, the supplier may make an up-front cash payment to the customer, by purchasing assets: equipment, land and buildings, staff resources. This may be a cash transaction or as a loan at a favourable rate, thereby generating more financial flexibility for the customer's corporate activities at the initial stage of outsourcing, by converting future capital expenditure on IT into regular service charges without the burden of their fixed overheads. This is a restricted and short term view of the potential benefits of outsourcing, but nevertheless may be of immense practical immediate benefit to certain customer organizations in straitened situations.

For a few customers in serious short term financial difficulties, the reasons for outsourcing may even be entirely financial, in restructuring their balance sheet and improving their cash flow. The supplier may creatively put together an attractive deal, postponing payments for services, injecting cash into the enterprise, and showing that tax gains may be realisable. Any other benefits in terms of efficiency, cheaper or improved services will be side effects. In this context, outsourcing can be construed merely as an imperative cost cutting exercise. Such customers should consider the ultimate value of short term financial gains and what is to happen when the contract comes to an end. The supplier will have to consider whether such a contractual relationship would be genuinely attractive.

Associated costs

The customer's budget for outsourcing IT must always include the costs of preparation for outsourcing, which can be surprisingly high. More than a decade ago it was reported[1] that expenditure by Customs and Excise came to two million pounds when it carried out its market test for computer services and professional consultancy services for a contract estimated at one hundred million pounds' worth of IT business. This included the costs of hiring consultants and the preparation work and bid evaluation. In this case the contract was eventually awarded to the in-house team.

The direct costs payable by the customer will include external professional fees such as those for outsourcing consultants and specialist legal advice, including drafting and negotiating the relevant contracts. There will also be internal management time and effort involved, from selecting the supplier through negotiating the commercial considerations to the execution and administration of the contract.

There will be the costs involved in communicating with potential suppliers, by open advertisements in the public sector or by means of direct contacts. The invitation to tender or other means of conveying information and asking for proposals must be prepared and distributed. The tenderers' resulting

---

1   *Computer Weekly*, 29th February 1996.

proposals must be evaluated, and the eventual selection made. There will be direct costs associated with transferring assets and resources, and in obtaining the necessary rights for the use of the licensed software by the supplier, whether by assignment or otherwise. Indirect costs of time will be involved in agreeing service levels and effort expended in keeping end users informed and contented.

In budgeting for the operation of the contract, unanticipated costs in the service provision should always be allowed for in addition to the charges estimated for the services. There will also be the costs of liaison management, contract management, audit and other residual costs for those functions retained in-house.

'In virtually every supplier-written contract we studied, we uncovered hidden costs, some adding up to hundreds of thousands – even millions – of dollars'.[2] Hopefully, the lessons have been learned from this pessimistic warning given several years ago, and the customer will be drawing up a customised contract to meet its own individual requirements.

The supplier's perspective

A supplier is carrying out outsourcing with a view to making a profit, and it is in its customers' interests that it should do so. A supplier operating on tight margins will not be able to make improvements or to innovate in its service provision.

The supplier will get no value out of a contract taken on purely because it has made the cheapest bid competitively without considering its profitability requirements. In order to do this, various associated indirect factors must be taken into account in calculating the contract price.

Indirectly there will be the costs of the supplier's unsuccessful bids for outsourcing contracts. One gained from six attempts is likely to be a good rate. One out of ten is probably more typical. General sales and marketing promotional expenses should not be underestimated. Long term cash flow has to be considered. At the outset of an outsourcing relationship, the supplier will have made a significant investment in taking over the installation, moving workloads to another machine, perhaps setting up at another site, taking on the customer's staff. It may have to look long term at making the greater part of its

---

2   'IT Outsourcing: Maximise Flexibility and Control', Lacity, Willcocks and Feeny, Harvard *Business Review*, May–June 1995.

profit in later years by achieving operating efficiency and price performance in its service provision. The supplier may need to invest in technology, other assets, training or other human resource benefits, during the term of the contract.

Suppliers do not appear to be differentiated primarily on charges, although significant differences do arise in individual responses to an invitation to tender. Within a reasonable range of varying charges, the customer's final selection of a supplier tends to be influenced by other characteristics of the proposals and presentations.

It may take eighteen months or more for outsourcing transactions to start generating revenue for the supplier, and the charges calculation will take this into account. A longer term for the contract will help to spread the cost of their initial investment.

Invitation to tender

The invitation to tender may be highly specific in seeking a fixed charging structure over the term of the contract, or it may request innovative costing proposals, seeking flexibility in ways of reducing costs and adding value. Inflation, productivity and efficiency improvements should be addressed. Joint ventures are discussed in Chapter 2. In the invitation to tender, the customer may ask for proposals from suppliers for creating joint ventures.

Tenderers should be asked to make it clear what is being excluded from their proposals and what assumptions they are making, to ensure that comparisons are being made on a fair basis. For example, they may be assuming a given level of inflation over the contract term. They may anticipate that licence fees will be separately negotiated. Their charges may be based on the customer accepting all the services from a single supplier rather than splitting up the services among a number of suppliers. Certain third party expenses may be part of the costs or may be separate. If the service costs are split into distinct areas of services, the customer's evaluation of the bids will be made easier. The bids should include details of additional charges such as payments to third parties, and how transferred assets will be paid for.

Where the main costs are to be fixed, development may also be treated as part of the core service up to a fixed number of hours or days, and then at a daily resource rate outside the core service.

Charging bases

The services may be provided at a fixed price or at a rate based on time, activity or volumes, and may extend to cost plus profit element for the supplier, open book accounting or reward sharing. There may well be a combination of different charging methods covering different parts of the services. The trends today are towards open book accounting and shared risk/rewards.

On start-up, an initial payment may be made by the customer to the supplier for the transfer of the services to the supplier. It may sometimes be a sum paid by the supplier to the customer, for the acquisition of hardware assets from the customer, or on the transfer of staff by the customer.

The supplier's service charges will comprise a number of elements: regular payments for the services, some incidentals and also direct costs. Recurring charges will be for the delivery of services, and it is up to the supplier how the resources should be managed to make a profit from the charges levied. There may be an agreed aim that resources should be gradually reduced over the contract term to achieve greater efficiencies and lower fixed costs. The charges may be expressed as unit costs or broken down in a number of ways according to various formulae or related to performance parameters, such as operating hours or workloads.

The customer will need to recognize that there will be a trade off between costs and service. Suppliers will implement cost control measures to save costs. They may have loss-leading first year contracts which rise in subsequent years or where the fixed price does not cover services which are bound to be needed at added prices. Sometimes users become more selective in justifying their requirements when the relation between payment and service provision becomes apparent. It may happen that a lower level of services than those expected when the services were provided in-house will become acceptable to end users, and that changes will cost more to implement.

In any method of charging, the supplier may require the customer to commit to an agreed overall minimum payment, in the knowledge that the individual volumes or percentages may fluctuate.

The customer may request a warning if a specific charging limit is likely to be exceeded. Normally any charging methodology will incorporate a system allowing rebates to the service charges, by service credits or by liquidated damages payable for failure to reach service levels. This is discussed in Chapter 4.

Fixed price

A fixed price provided by an outsourcing supplier will seem an attractive prospect to a Board whose members are unsympathetic to the difficulties of forecasting the costs of IT, yet who are conscious that such costs always seem to be increasing.

In its simplest form, this is a price agreed between the supplier and the customer for the provision of services during the term of the contract. It may be expressed as an annual charge for each of the years of the contract's life.

The customer's Board members may assume that a fixed price costing will give the benefits of certainty. If this is to be the case, and indeed for this kind of pricing arrangement to be appropriate, the contract must be short term, or one in which the services, deliverables and volumes themselves can be accurately predicted and controlled. It is suitable where the requirements are well defined, and where no changes are envisaged. It might be used when an obsolescent system likely to be of short term duration is being handed over for outsourcing until its replacement becomes fully operational, or for systems which are self-contained or which have very limited interaction with other systems.

The contract may recognise the specific circumstances in which the fixed price will be increased as a result of changed or increased activities and volumes, or the introduction of new technology, and it may be linked to price inflation indexation.

For the supplier, a fixed price will bring predictable revenues, subject to the risk that the fixed price will not cover all the elements involved in the services. The supplier may adjust its service delivery to retain its profit margin if the costs of providing the service increase because of factors outside its control. This leads to risks for the customer that the levels of services deteriorate and that variations will cost more to implement. This is allied to the view that 'there is no such thing as a fixed price contract', because there will always be unforeseen circumstances and changes required. Higher prices may then apply to subsequent amendments to the services agreed on a time and materials basis.

In practice with a fixed price contract, what is most likely to happen is that there will be a basic banded fixed price or a minimum charge together with a rate which changes according to the varying number of users or employees or accounts. This allows for change based on agreed procedures. There may be a unit charge per transaction or per user to allow for varying volumes, or an overall charge for a limited volume with variations agreed for percentage or actual increases or significant shortfalls. It may be agreed to carry out the adjustments retrospectively following the calculations, or predicted changes may be agreed in advance and reconciled later.

Time and materials

In this arrangement, payment is by unit pricing according to actual usage. The usage might be of various kinds of resources, ranging from computer time to human resources.

Connect time to the computer is one form of rate that can be measured easily, for example by machine time per second, or connect time per hour; storage costs in terms of media, length of time of storage and volumes.

The normal payment method for development and programming work or for other resource-based services would be at an hourly or daily resource rate according to seniority and experience, dependent on time spent.

The risk for the customer is that the charging method will be perceived to be open-ended. This risk can be contained by limits specified in the contract, such as estimated ceilings, or early warnings by the supplier of increases to the estimated costs, so that the customer has a choice, at least in principle, of whether to accept the higher charges or whether to prioritize or to forego some requirements. In practice, the choice may not be entirely open if the customer is dependent on the services.

The risk for the supplier is of uncertainty of income and use of resources: demand may fluctuate unexpectedly, with consequent difficulties in resourcing services where the requirements suddenly increase, or having superfluous overheads if requirements decline. There is little incentive with this method for the supplier to develop improvements in service delivery.

Open book procedures

With open book procedures the supplier must disclose to the customer information about the composition of the costs of running the services and its profits earned in providing them. What is agreed to be disclosed may cover equipment costs, software licences, profit margins, contributions to overheads, and staff salaries.

The charges will then consist of the costs actually incurred together with a management fee on top.

Open book charges are appropriate for costs which are going to vary. One example where these charges are often used, with or without management fees, is for staff costs, in particular for contract staff used on development work. Another is for exploiting other assets which have been transferred, perhaps at a nominal amount, such as equipment or for capacity usage.

Sharing profits or savings

By extension to open book procedures, profits or savings may be shared. The supplier may take an agreed percentage as profit. If the profits turn out to be greater than expected, the difference will be split between supplier and customer. Alternatively the basis for sharing the difference may be the calculation of improvements made to the customer's revenues or margins. Naturally the formulae selected must be measurable, both parties must be willing to co-operate, and the supplier must be prepared to make the information available.

A budget for some or all of the costs or a target price may be agreed between the supplier and the customer at the start of each year of the contract. The actual costs will be ascertained through audit. Resulting savings made beyond that may be shared equally or on some other basis.

For example, incentives may be agreed in the contract by creating formulae for establishing when reductions in staff costs or service delivery are achieved, so that where ongoing savings are realized, the savings are allocated proportionately.

If the supplier's actual costs plus agreed margin exceed the target price, so that the savings from the contract for the customer are less than anticipated, the supplier will also take a loss, the shortfall being shared between the parties in the agreed proportions. If the supplier's actual costs plus agreed margin are less than the target price, the gain will be shared. The contract will detail the potential costs overrun or gain which the customer and supplier agree. This gives the supplier an incentive to keep the costs down and to work to the targets. However, if the supplier's costs are less than the target price, the customer is paying a percentage of the difference between the actual costs and the target price, and obtaining less benefit than on a unit priced, time and materials basis. The costs payable by the customer may not be predictable and the administration can be complicated.

In principle the customer may challenge the costs or profits. In practice it is not easy for an external party to assess the cost of the supplier's administrative overheads and their allocation to any single customer.

Nevertheless these charging methods can act as an incentive for the supplier and will benefit both parties where the services are amenable to improvement.

In fact there is likely to be a combination of charging methods.

Ancillary expenses and charges

Some third party charges may be payable by the customer, either directly to the third party or via the supplier, such as contractors' charges, third party licence charges, hardware maintenance and software support. The supplier may take a fee for the costs of administration. Other costs which arise from time to time, such as training courses, may also be charged for additionally and directly.

The contract should define what expenses may be claimed, and what are excluded; and when agreement in advance is required before expenses may be claimed. The production of receipts for actual expenditure may be a requirement. Should travel by the supplier's staff to the customer's sites be allowable as expenses? When is hotel accommodation permissible? Would attendance at meetings called by the customer over and above the contractual review procedures attract expenses for the supplier's senior staff? What about charges for time spent in responding to third party auditors' questions?

Variations to the charges

The review of charges is important. In all but the simplest short term fixed price contract with no scope for extension, procedures and parameters for varying the charges should be stated. A supplier has to keep pace with rates of inflation and, in particular, with salary increases in the IT industry. It must have the right to increase its charges at some point, unless its quote has been purely on the basis of a fixed price or rate for a limited time.

However, some contractual control should be exercised by the customer over rates of increases which are acceptable, so that the supplier does not have unfettered power to control the charges it makes.

There should be a set period from the commencement of the contract during which the charges will not be increased. Thereafter, increases should be allowed only at limited intervals – such as not more frequently than at twelve-month intervals – and confined to a reasonable level. This may be done by linking increases to inflation by means of an appropriate index, such as the Retail Prices Index. Since staff salaries are such a significant part of the outsourcing provider's budget, a computer salaries index may be more relevant. For over twenty years the National Computing Centre has been carrying out annual surveys of the UK IT labour market across job categories and industry sectors – the *Benchmark of Salaries and Employment Trends in IT* – to provide an analysis of IT salary levels and IT employment trends.[3] Computer Economics,[4] a research and advisory organization for strategic and financial management of information systems, publishes the annual reports *Computer Economics IT Salary Report* and *Spending, Staffing and Technology Trends*.

While limiting how the charges may be increased, it is to be anticipated that some running costs should decrease over the term of the contract. The unit costs of IT drop exponentially over time. Old legacy systems can be replaced with lower cost hardware and software packages.

If customers do not appreciate this, they will be paying the same fees over the contract term and not gaining from potential savings.

Any variation to the services may carry cost implications. The change control procedure is described in Chapter 10, and any increased charges as a result of the variation must be agreed in advance of proceeding with the change.

Payment methods

How the supplier is to be paid will affect its cash flow and will therefore indirectly impact its charges. The recurring payments for service provision may be made at monthly or quarterly intervals, or by instalments, and in advance or in arrears. There may need to be end-of-year reconciliations where payments were made on the basis of estimates. Expenses and non-recurring agreed charges are typically paid for in arrears, monthly or quarterly.

VAT will be payable by the customer to the supplier in addition to the charges, and there must be a statement in the contract to this effect. For offshore contracts, the position on VAT must be checked.

---

3 http://www.nccshop.co.uk/mall/productpage.cfm/NCC/P-SURSAL2008.
4 http://www.computereconomics.com.

It is reasonable for the supplier to minimise its risk of non-payment or late payment by reserving the right to charge interest in the event of late payment. The supplier may claim statutory interest on the debt, currently the Bank of England base rate plus eight per cent. This rate is set each half-year in June and December for the following six months. The supplier may choose not to enforce the payment of interest, for example if the relationship is generally satisfactory and late payment by the customer has occurred inadvertently only on one occasion.

The supplier may also wish to include a provision for suspension or termination of the service in the event of non-payment. The customer may negotiate for this to follow a formal notice giving a number of days' grace, in case it is merely due to an administrative error that the payment has not been made. Services important to running the business should not be suspended without warning. However, suspension may be a reasonable lever for the supplier whose payments are consistently delayed.

If a dispute arises, the customer may seek to suspend payments. If negotiations to resolve the dispute are in progress, there can be a provision in the contract for the payments relating to the matter in dispute to be made to an interest-bearing deposit account in the parties' joint names. Following resolution of the dispute the sum can be paid out to the parties as agreed by the settlement, and interest allocated pro rata according to the distribution of the principal sum.

Monitoring charges

To discover whether benefits which it was assumed would be achieved following the move to outsourcing are in fact being realized, the customer should be monitoring the charges as well as the service levels, in order to obtain a true picture of the value of the outsourcing services over the life of the contract.

This monitoring may take place at a number of levels. The ongoing costs should be compared from time to time with the costs predicted at the outset by the supplier and as estimated by the customer. It may be salutary to recall the in-house budget plans, had outsourcing not proceeded.

It may be possible to benchmark services against similar services provided to organizations which are equivalent to the customer's, in terms of size and complexity – if any can be found. The supplier's charges for the services, or for some selected services, are reviewed against a comparable supplier for similar services. Where it is difficult to agree on comparable organizations overall, it may be possible to break down the services and related charges into discrete categories for individual comparisons to be made. This will not be entirely satisfactory, as various allowances will have to be built into the assessments.

Various commercial performance benchmark indices are available, such as categories of unit costs. Market surveys may also be commissioned and paid for by the customer, or jointly by the parties, to assess performance of those services whose costs are being measured but for which there are no criteria.

The results of the monitoring carried out from time to time should be tabled for discussion at a review meeting. If an objective analysis and comparison can be made to establish the value being obtained from outsourcing, this will provide an informed basis for ascertaining whether the outsourcing is a qualified success or unmitigated failure. It should be agreed in the contract that where there are shortcomings, plans should be drawn up and agreed within a specified time, for the purpose of improving the services and adjusting the charges.

Clauses on charges and costings should be negotiated by the customer with the objective of confirming value for money throughout the period of the contract.

Management Liaison and Review

'In many cases, the value of outsourcing is not maximised because senior executives critically under-estimate the level of management resource needed to both implement and sustain a successful outsourcing initiative over time.'[1]

Once the outsourcing contract has come into effect, the management of the continuing relationship between supplier and customer is of enormous importance. The mechanisms for the liaison between customer and supplier should be discussed when the contract is being negotiated. A clear understanding of the separate functions and roles of each party and the divisions between them is essential and should be set out formally and in detail in the contract. This is all part of the balance of co-operation and control.

Customer management

It is easy to underestimate the customer management responsibilities that will continue to exist under an IT outsourcing arrangement. Control is a fundamental part of a customer's ability to retain leverage over the supplier, whose own legitimate objectives include being in the business in order to make a profit. It is not enough for the customer only to note at the time of paying the invoices, that the services continue in general to be provided. It is not adequate merely to check that the bills relate approximately to the volumes and response times specified as the service levels. The outsourcing must be coherently managed by the customer, in order to be efficient and to be an effective part of the customer's overall business strategy. There is a need for this management to be entrusted to one or more persons with sufficient calibre and professional competence at least equivalent to the supplier's.

For other bought-in services, overall supervision is normal. Any externally provided services such as marketing campaigns or transportation will be

---

1   'Why, when and how to outsource', David Muir, *Computer Weekly*, 3 October 2006.

carried out with some involvement and decision making by the customer organization's director or line manager responsible, or by a management team brought together especially for the purpose. These other services may be relatively simple to provide. They may comprise an individual activity, such as by instructing a firm of solicitors to act on a one-off employment dispute. They may be for a single function, for example for catering services. They may last for a matter of weeks or months, and be easier to discard if performance is erratic or otherwise ineffective. Outsourcing IT services are continuous, more pervasive, and will last longer. It is therefore vital for the customer to be aware of how the services are being carried out, and to ensure that they will continue to meet its requirements, even in changing circumstances.

The customer will need a budget for this, which should include those areas which have not been outsourced – for instance a budget for research and development if the outsourcing provider is not acting as an agent of change, but dealing with operational IT. It may cost up to ten per cent of the contract value to manage it effectively.

The customer's management of outsourced services will cover three main areas: responsibility for assessing current performance; prioritizing future requirements; and controlling variations, in the customer's business context for the services which are being provided, to the agreed standards, for the price being paid. Without this management capability, a customer will have no means of knowing if the charges are reasonable or whether the service levels are being satisfactorily sustained.

The customer will therefore take a range of considerations into account in its control and planning. The demands of end users and the existing relationship with them, successful co-ordination of all the different systems, the customer's business policy and future requirements, its cultural style, have all to be combined.

It follows that division of the responsibilities should entail the supplier running and managing the services and the control of their delivery, while the customer manages the integration of the services with the strategic direction of its business. The customer must retain ultimate responsibility for making its business decisions, and for its IT strategy. It should be willing to be guided in this by the advice or recommendations of the outsourcing supplier or by third party consultants.

Within this basic division between supplier and customer, however, the extent of control retained by the customer should be a matter for negotiation.

For example, in one telecommunications outsourcing of corporate wide area voice and data networks, the supplier had extensive commitments covering infrastructure management, migration and a high level of user project management. The customer's in-house core team retained the overall architecture, and consequently took charge of controlling strategy, standards and security. However, the supplier was encouraged to contribute to these areas, especially in seeking new network capabilities and services.

In another case, in an outsourcing by a manufacturer of its commercial IT operations together with some development work, hardware maintenance and network management for its factories, it was the manufacturer's in-house team which established the policies and procedures, dealt with the management of the contract and service level agreement, and with the interface between end users and suppliers.

If the customer has the resources to do so, it may wish to take a more interventionist approach. Some companies may have their reasons for retaining control over the final selection of replacement hardware and software. For example, are all third party payments to be made directly by the supplier?

Depending on the nature of the outsourcing, the supplier may require the customer to accept responsibility for preparation and accuracy of its own data, notification of any special features and delivery to an agreed time scale. Then if, for instance, the system outputs are not delivered in time or properly, and this is as a direct result of the customer's inadequate data, the supplier will not be liable.

The existing IT management function will therefore change once the outsourcing process starts, as different skills will be invoked for the new liaison management role. The customer will no longer have a requirement for extensive technical IT expertise or for general IT staff management experience. The customer should therefore budget to allow for an in-house function, however much reduced in amount.

Although there is no longer a need to have the same range of technical skills as before, the customer will be well advised to retain – or acquire – enough technical capability in-house, for understanding the operation of the contracted services, to recognise technological innovations in the customer's market sector, to know how to cope with changes in demand from users, and to appreciate whether technical failures are being properly resolved. One statement of the ideal, made several years ago but still valid, is:

> 'Retain just enough in-house expertise to check up on supplier performance, keep up with technical issues and devise the next strategy.[2]

General management abilities, negotiating skills, common-sense and judgement, and financial understanding are also desirable to derive the best from the outsourcing, in order to be able to solve any problems within the contractual framework, while keeping the relationships amicable yet professional.

This is not to say that it will inevitably be the same members of the customer's existing IT management team who will be tasked with the liaison management. In any event it may be that there is no single person or combination of people employed by the customer with all the attributes suitable for taking on the new role.

It may therefore be necessary to make new appointments, of a liaison services manager, consultant or team from outside, for managing the liaison process and adding value, without duplicating the outsourcer's work. Such appointments must be independent of any particular vendor or service provider, and be of personnel who understand the customer's sector or industry, have the appropriate combination of technical, business and commercial skills, experience in building relationships at all levels of the outsourcing, and in liaising with a range of vendors and providers to ensure that they work effectively together.

This liaison person or team must be familiar with the details of the outsourcing agreement and understand all its implications. It must not micro-manage the outsourcer by constant monitoring, which would be regarded as interference by the outsourcer, with some justification, and would engender an atmosphere of distrust.

For the process to be effective, there should be a direct reporting channel at the customer's Board level (or its equivalent where the organizational structure is not a corporate one), whether the liaison services role is an internal or an external service function in the customer organization.

---

2   Richard Brett, *MBA Newsletter*, July 1995.

Representatives and liaison

Representatives should be appointed by each party, by the supplier as well as by the customer. They will each play a key part in the liaison process. The responsibilities of each will differ, but both should have sufficient authority to be able to act and take decisions on behalf of their respective organizations, and to be able to give or receive information required by the other. Each representative needs to be more than a figurehead liaison officer without any real power to influence the course of events. This is particularly evident when decisions need to be made quickly in the light of the performance of the services or their variation or in adding to them, to keep the arrangement on course or to overcome deviations.

The individual roles of the representatives will influence the titles they are to be given, whether they are to be regarded as account manager, project manager or contract manager. It is recommended for convenience that the customer representative should have a different title from the supplier representative. They will have different functions and it will be easier to draft the contract and to understand it from the representatives' respective perspectives and roles. For a large outsourcing project a steering team for either or both parties may be necessary, with responsibilities shared among the members.

Each party may wish to have some say in the appointment or any replacement of the other party's senior representatives, as the people in these roles will work closely together and will be vital to the success of the outsourcing relationship. Tension may arise in the negotiations if the customer expects to be able to participate in the choice of successors to any staff of the supplier who leave, other than the personnel agreed as key to the outsourcing functions.

If the supplier and customer representatives were not able to work together, this would cause major difficulties. For a major outsourcing, the customer may reasonably expect to have some say in the appointment of the supplier's representative. The argument may be extended to having designated representatives named in a schedule to the contract, who have been agreed by the customer or by both parties. Curriculum vitae may be asked for on the appointment or replacement of individuals. If this is agreed, some reasonable parameters need to be set, so that there is no arbitrary exclusion. There may have to be procedures agreed in the selection of a replacement, and time allowed for the process.

It may happen that one particular individual is crucial to the decision by the customer in the selection of a supplier. For example, in a small supplier company the managing director may be taking a keen personal interest in the success of the outsourcing. That person may be named as key to the contract, but in the interests of both parties, the extent of that indispensability needs to be agreed, and the contract must be able to survive any individual move or transfer.

Consideration should be given to channelling all communications concerning the performance through the nominated representatives. Care would be needed about this in operation. If it is decided that this would be a desirable method of working, deputies should also be nominated so that there is always a decision maker available. There is certainly a need to channel day-to-day operational liaison so as to prevent a possible cacophony of conflicting voices, and also to avoid obstructing necessary communications.

The description of the liaison role will include a number of activities for each party, such as those listed below. These activities may form part of a job description, and some could be specified as contractual requirements. However, they will not all be appropriate for both supplier and customer representatives, and it would not normally be essential or even desirable to make them contractually so specific. It may be wise not to be to dogmatic.

SERVICES AND MONITORING

- assessing contract performance, by monitoring the services against the contract and against the service levels agreed;

- resolving inadequacies in existing services;

- monitoring security and contingency procedures;

- reviewing the accuracy of documentation, especially after variations to the services have been introduced;

- monitoring change control procedures;

- providing regular statistics and reports;

- interpreting and reviewing the reports and statistics;

- audit rights.

CONTRACT

- keeping the contract, its schedules and appendices, and service level agreements up to date;

- keeping staff informed as necessary of the contractual commitments – for example, concerning confidentiality, agreed turn round times, payment schedules.

COMMUNICATION

- managing demand for the services;

- communicating with end users, getting feedback on a formal basis and ensuring that their needs are addressed within the contract constraints;

- identifying and addressing training needs of staff – customer's, supplier's, end users';

- attending, organizing, minuting, running the liaison meetings;

- co-operating with the other party's representative.

PLANNING

- articulating variations;

- identifying possible or necessary new services;

- long term strategy;

- contract re-negotiation.

CO-ORDINATION

- For selective sourcing, the customer may need to co-ordinate the different suppliers' work, ensuring clear boundaries of responsibility of individual input and task completion relative to other suppliers.

- Overall technical and financial knowledge must be co-ordinated with those staff who hold key responsibilities in these areas.

Managing the end user relationship

If end users are involved in the outsourcing, they must have a channel for communicating their requirements. If there are many end users or if there are different kinds of end users, some co-ordination will be necessary. This may be through the customer representative or it may be appropriate for the end users to interact directly with the supplier. The choice of communication route will be influenced by how variations affecting end users are to be introduced; how the charges made by the supplier relate to the usage by end users; and the relationship of the customer management with its end users.

In providing the services, the supplier may be close to the end users, and in a position to recommend attractive new solutions which will require further expenditure by the customer. To control this, the customer may establish a designated procedure for channelling end user requests for more resources or updated technology via the customer's representative.

Once the contract is in effect, end users will be alert in critically noticing any differences in the service provision from what they were previously receiving. The tasks of the customer's representative should include regular liaison with end users, in order to learn promptly of any operational problems or new ideas, so that action may be taken wherever possible to remedy or enhance the service provision.

Co-operation and good will are essential in outsourcing as in IT arrangements generally, but this need not be at the expense of objective ongoing analysis and assessment which will be critical to long term success. This assessment can be effected by having formal meetings and procedures for reviewing service level statistics of performance and results, and other reports. Each party should draw up its own internal procedures to reflect its own responsibilities in this respect.

Reports and statistics

The supplier's principal responsibility is to carry out the services as stipulated in the contract, and there should be willingness to demonstrate this in practice to the customer. To assist in this, regular reports and statistics will be a contractual requirement. The supplier will be expected to produce performance reports to show compliance with service levels, exception reports, trend analyses and charts, and various other reports and statistics, monthly or quarterly. Nevertheless, it must be remembered that the supplier's effort in producing the paperwork to report and substantiate the provision of the services will be reflected in the overall costs of the services. It is therefore worth spending time when the contract is being negotiated in agreeing what methods will be the most useful for assessing the effectiveness of the service provision.

The manner of presenting the performance reports should be agreed, but not necessarily crystallized as part of the contractual terms. If the reports are found to be useful in practice, better ways of making them still more effective may be requested by the customer.

The contract or associated procedures should stipulate when the reports are to be made available, particularly so as to allow time for perusal in advance of any meetings where they are to be the subject of discussion.

Meetings and reviews

The outsourcing customer needs a structured method of monitoring and reviewing the services. There is nothing new about this. In Barbara Tuchman's account of the calamitous fourteenth century,[3] she describes the review or *montre* for knights and squires in war service to their ruler. In those days armies had little structure with no proper hierarchy of command. There were standard rates of pay for nobles according to status, and the King had to ensure that he was getting the level of quality for which he was paying. Generally the review would take place monthly by officials on the lookout for valets being substituted for their masters, vigilant to detect whether healthy horses presented for their approval would be replaced by old nags for battle.

A framework of formal meetings and reviews, and the ways in which they will operate, should be set out in the contract. Depending on the complexity of the outsourcing, there may be several review levels. For example, if the size of the outsourcing justifies it, there may be three types of meetings:

1.   a business management meeting to monitor the contract;

2.   an operational review meeting to plan and monitor services;

3.   functional steering group meetings established for strategic planning.

---

3   Barbara W Tuchman, *A Distant Mirror*, Macmillan, 1978.

This means first that decisions need to be taken on what different kinds of review points should be established, for what functions. Then, how often should the meetings take place? How prescriptive should their format be? How far should their administrative procedures be elaborated as a basis for successful checks and balances over the life of the contract?

The regular operational meeting is the minimum level of management review. The appointed representatives of each party, together with other members of the teams involved if this is appropriate, should meet regularly, perhaps monthly as a good starting point, possibly more frequently at the outset. This should not inhibit normal day-to-day informal discussion of progress by the representatives between meetings – by email or telephone as well as face-to-face.

The primary focus of these meetings will be to review the service levels through consideration of the key performance indicator figures. At the same time any unusual incidents or events since the previous meeting should be reported and assessed. The progress of any agreed developments, enhancements or other modifications should be evaluated.

Reports and statistics required from the supplier as part of the overall review process should be listed in the contract, and whether they are to be produced for every meeting or at less frequent intervals; and how far in advance of the meeting they should be available. At best there will be confirmation that all is working as anticipated. If service levels are related to payment, this will be material for justifying submission of the supplier's invoices.

Adverse trends can be identified and appropriate action initiated. In this way the meetings can be an early warning system, ideally a means of foreseeing problems to obviate them. Of course the meeting will also be the forum for creating positive solutions to problems which have already arisen.

At these meetings, variations to the services may be proposed and negotiated. Either party may suggest ways of enhancing, adding value to, increasing or decreasing the scope of the services.

When there are no alarms, all is apparently running smoothly, and it becomes difficult to find mutually agreeable dates for the meetings, they should still continue to be held at the agreed intervals. They should remain the focal point for raising any issues or for discussing exceptions. In their absence a false sense of security may easily be engendered. Unanticipated problems may gradually emerge, or unresolved tensions or resentment may build up, which a short airing would have solved. Continuing personal interaction is important.

The meetings should reinforce the spirit of co-operation between the representatives, and therefore collaborative effort between the supplier and customer's staff as a whole. Nevertheless, both representatives must remember that they hold their positions on behalf of their respective organizations and their interests are therefore not identical. Within the scope of the contract it cannot be assumed that all will be bound to be well in the best of all possible worlds.

Responsibility should be allocated for drawing up the agenda. It may include:

- confirmation of notes of the previous meeting, follow up of actions taken, and discussion of matters arising not otherwise on the agenda;
- review and discussion of service performance against service level agreements;
- unusual incidents or events, or specific problems;
- administrative issues;
- proposed changes, requests for enhancements or modifications, or new services or products;
- progress on agreed changes, enhancements or modifications;
- any other business.

There is a strong argument in favour of the customer's representative chairing the meeting, as part of its fundamental control of outsourcing strategy.

One party should be in charge of preparing and distributing notes from the meeting, although they should be agreed by both parties. These notes should consist of records of what was agreed and commitments to be undertaken as actions arising from the meeting.

If the meeting notes are to be used actively as working documents, it can sometimes assist to have the reasons briefly summarized for the decisions taken. But confessionals are to be avoided. If problems do arise, it is not helpful to have a complete account of the candid exchange of views which may have occurred at the meeting. It is not unknown for such minutes to become an embarrassing permanent record of senior members of staff bewailing the poor quality of their own products or services or lack of control.

At the next level up from the standard progress meetings, strategic reviews will be required less regularly: quarterly, six-monthly or annually. The emphasis will be away from the practicalities of normal monitoring and administrative processes. The objective will be to consider whether any new business directions will affect the scope and provision of the services, and any ways in which the services can be streamlined, adapted and improved to give better value. It will be useful to note whether decisions are being taken at the right level and whether senior management is being involved too often or too little. Are problems normally being sorted out satisfactorily with not too much bureaucracy, but with a record of what was agreed? These reviews will typically be conducted at Board or senior management level for each party, that is to say, by officials who are at some remove from any immediate practical role, although the senior outsourcing representatives will also participate.

For reference purposes, the formats for the meetings and strategic reviews, listing the personnel taking part and the procedures to be followed, should be recorded in a document which can be physically accessed independently of the contract, perhaps in the form of a schedule.

The control exercised by the customer through meetings and reviews may be tighter at the start of the relationship, at a time when the informal mechanisms are not yet established, when it may not be clear whether the service levels will all be realistic, when there may be apprehension on the part of the customer, and when the supplier may not yet have become familiar with the customer's systems. However, if the regulatory mechanisms should loosen, this should be as a result of a deliberate decision by the customer, not on account of indolence.

Finally if there is a steering committee for IT governance, consisting of very senior executives of each party, it will meet at pre-defined points during the life of the contract, perhaps annually, with the option of convening at other times if there is a problem being escalated. This committee meets to ensure that IT strategy and architecture are aligned with the customer's business strategy. There may be more customer than supplier representatives on this committee. It should ensure that innovation is not ignored, and that new technology can be exploited for changing business needs in the outsourcing services.

Escalation procedures

When representatives are appointed, responsibilities allocated and procedures established, problems will be minimised, but this provides no guarantee that they will be avoided altogether. Wherever complicated affairs are being managed, in the normal course of events differences can be expected to emerge from time to time between supplier and customer. It is nevertheless disheartening when conflicts do arise, whether these are through perceived inadequacies in communication or in carrying out the service activities or because of different perceptions, or over other apparent shortcomings.

Where different groups of people are working together over a period of time, problems can emerge from trivial causes. Experienced managers should be able to handle many potential confrontations, where areas of responsibilities, chains of command and reporting structures have been put in place. For example, consultants from companies who would have liked to win the outsourcing work but who failed in their bids, may be working alongside the supplier's staff. A contractual commitment should be given by the supplier that it will co-operate with any third party contractors providing services to the customer.

The meetings which have been set up will be the normal forum at which complaints may be raised and resulting courses of action proposed. Yet there will be occasions when the normal channels for communication and reporting will not work satisfactorily. To allow for this, an escalation procedure should be set out in the contract. At times of controversy, the known channels for attempting to resolve disagreements can be adopted sooner rather than later, with a view to clearing the problem out of the way and getting back to the primary purpose of running the contract.

Unresolved problems will be referred up to senior decision makers not immediately involved. They will have a perspective distanced from the daily involvement in the services, which can often make solutions to problems easier to reach.

The escalation procedure should define the point at which the next level of authority will be invoked. This may be triggered within a specified time span, whether days or even hours according to the seriousness of the predicament, or through the general meetings and strategic reviews in the first instance. A number of tiers may be agreed, up to to the steering committee for IT governance if one has been set up, or referral to Board level or its equivalent for both organizations, with final appeal to an expert or arbitrator. Methods of formal dispute resolution for breach of contract if the escalation procedures do not succeed are discussed in Chapter 13.

The overriding object is to clear any problem out of the way by sorting it out in order to carry on with the outsourcing process and preferably to keep a positive working relationship.

Independent audit

The contract should allow for periodic audits to be carried out. An 'audit' used simply to be a financial audit to check that all sums were accounted for and that no fraud was taking place. Now the term is more widely used for various reviews or checks and even for collecting and collating information. For monitoring and review of the outsourcing, both internal and external audits may be called for.

The ISO 9001:2008 standard[4] is used for certification and registration purposes by organizations in relation to their quality management systems. Those organizations which are accredited with ISO 9001:2008 will already be familiar with internal and external audits to demonstrate continuing compliance with formal procedures.

It may be that the customer organization already employs internal auditors for reviewing its systems. The primary UK professional body for internal auditors is the Institute of Internal Auditors,[5] which represents, promotes and develops the professional practice of internal auditing, and provides professional qualifications. However, internal auditors may have other qualifications or have been appointed by virtue of experience gained within the organization through familiarity with its business practices or elsewhere.

For an external review of the outsourcing processes, an independent auditor on behalf of the customer must be acceptable to the outsourcing provider. For example, chartered accountants are recognised under the Companies Acts as qualified to be auditors by virtue of their training. Chartered information system professionals will also have the competence to undertake external audits. The external auditor will provide a professional opinion, reporting on the findings of compliance with service levels and performance standards, and where relevant, that the correct charges have been imposed.

---

4   http://www.iso.org/iso/catalogue_detail?csnumber=46486.
5   http://www.iia.org.uk/.

The details of control of the outsourcing by the deployment of representatives, meeting schedules and formalities, statistics and reports required should therefore be set out in the contract, the balance of control lying with the customer, who must retain at senior level the responsibility for the strategic and planning focus. It is the customer's job to ensure that the IT services continue to meet the needs of its business, to promote IT in its business, and to maintain the investment – allowing for changes in technology. The customer cannot discard its evaluation and decision making capability. It must still take decisions about business development and systems integration. It must be seen to be managing the contract.

Allowing for Change

CHAPTER

10

Change is integral to the IT industry. For any decision taken on which hardware, software, system or services to buy, or about which skills to send employees on training courses to acquire, six months later there will be more options available with different, more versatile and cheaper new offerings in the market. Like IT professionals, a number of Alan Coren's university contemporaries in the Foreign Office found themselves in this state which he described as 'permanent dynamic obsolescence'. If they had read Japanese, they were given a special training course to learn German, and subsequently posted to Kampala. If they were commercially brilliant, they were despatched where political expertise was the sole requirement. If they were geographers, they were given posts to advise on chicken diseases. It seemed as if, as soon as they had completed the long and arduous process of learning something, it was no longer required.[1]

The environment of the IT outsourcing contract is as subject to change as the general business environment in which the customer organization operates. The IT outsourcing relationship itself is usually intended to develop, to allow for these environmental dynamics, the customer's changing requirements and technology advances. Some flexibility in the provision of services may be built into the contract, but this will not always prevent other modifications being required or requested, perhaps to achieve a more effective result or to extend the scope of the services. A procedure for enabling variations to be made during the term of the outsourcing agreement needs to be built into the contract, to define precisely what constitutes a 'change' as opposed to what is expected within the outsourcing service provision, to record the change, to enable the process of change to be controlled, including the price to be charged, and so that the variation may be incorporated as a contractual amendment. It is easy for an apparently simple change to be agreed without appreciating the implications that may arise. Any proposed change should be considered properly before implementation so that all its consequences may be taken into account.

---

1   Alan Coren, *The Sanity Inspector*, Coronet Books, 1974.

Both parties must be clear about who is entitled to instigate the proposal for change, whether either party is an a position to choose to accept or reject the change, and how control over the process of making the change is to be maintained.

For an outsourcing contract entered into for obsolescent systems, a change control procedure will probably not be necessary. The contract will be for known requirements, to cover a limited period until the customer's replacement systems are up and running. Nor will it necessarily apply in the case of other selective outsourcing contracts of limited scope, for a single system or for a short duration. In other circumstances, however, the procedure for handling requests for changes should be part of the contract management processes.

For outsourcing transactions where the whole purpose comprises the fundamental organizational changes of business transformation or re-engineering by the supplier, with concomitantly greater risk borne by both parties, with the customer's active participation and co-operation essential to the transformation activities, it will normally be more appropriate to draft and negotiate the contract for this objective, rather than to rely on change control procedures to vary the supplier's service provision.

Changes

The contract may categorize changes according to whether they are variations forming part of the normal service provision and included in the charges, or whether they should be dealt with by following the change control procedure.

Changes which may be implemented by the supplier in the ordinary course of events without recourse to change control procedures may include those for scalability, for example where the charges are automatically adjusted upwards or downwards according to variations to volume throughput. Or the service charges may allow for an annual figure budgeted for resource effort in hours or days, which might be used for minor development work or for small modifications. The definition of what counts as a change must exclude such anticipated improvements.

Changes which are not part of the normal provision of services and which fall within the change control procedure may be those necessary to cover revisions to standards or the regulatory environment with which the customer must comply, and changes in the law as a result of new legislation or case law decisions, where the customer has no choice about the implementation. Payroll is one example of a system which requires constant attention each year or more frequently, as the amounts vary, volumes fluctuate and tax laws change.

The customer may seek changes for greater convenience or for economy or because of altered requirements. The supplier may be able to recommend efficiency or quality changes, as it learns more about the customer's business, and to take advantage of new technology. The service levels initially agreed may be varied over the course of the contract term. Contractually provision should be made for formal review of the services from time to time, leading to new service requirements which may be put forward by either the customer or the supplier. Most frequently variations to the contract will mean relatively minor modifications to the services: for example, the number of reports which are required, and by what deadline. The contract must not be so stringently drawn that it becomes difficult to make even these kinds of administrative amendments.

Variations may be required as a result of technological advances or changes arising from business strategy shifts.

Technological changes

Access to advances in technology is one of the potential advantages of outsourcing. The supplier may achieve service level objectives by technological refresh through incremental updating, by bringing in upgrades in hardware, operating systems, software, communications in terms of processing power, storage capacity, new interfaces, and networks, as part of its services, by doing the same thing more cheaply or something better for the same price. Alternatively, any proposed innovatory change may have to be subject to scrutiny through the change control procedure. Technological changes may consist of radically different ways of delivering functionality, where the proposal and its costs have to be investigated. A procedure specifically for technology review may be built into the contract. This can be one of the functions of a strategic review committee, which meets in order to consider longer term improvements, not for day-to-day overseeing of the contract. The supplier may be charged with reporting to this committee from time to time on current market practices and trends, although it should remain open to the customer to carry out or commission its own review. In its recommendations, the supplier must understand whether the customer is characterized as an early adopter or, more likely, as prepared to move only to tried and tested technology solutions.

This may be formalised further. It may be a requirement of the contract that a regular general benchmarking exercise – or health check – is carried out on value for money of the outsourcing, with organizations comparable in terms of similar size, turnover and business function. Technology benchmarking can form part of this. Where this is a formal network of comparator organizations, it may be more acceptable to all for the information provided to be anonymized, and care must be taken to avoid any implications of price fixing or other abuse of competition law. Benchmarking is discussed further in Chapter 8.

Business strategy changes

Having entered into the outsourcing, the customer may be expecting to avoid major upheaval. Yet the possibility of enhancements and development to bring about significant changes in the services, should not be discounted simply because such variations had not been foreseen when the contract was being negotiated.

Companies change direction, re-organize, realign and rearrange their priorities. They strive to keep their competitive edge. They may do this by specializing or by diversifying, by changes in top management, by restructuring management hierarchies, by introducing a new management philosophy, by looking outwards on a global basis or by cutting out non-core activities. Any of these activities will directly affect the IT resources they need and will be reflected in consequent changes to the way the outsourcing services are provided, or to other aspects of the contract.

This may be so even where the contract is for a non-core application. For example, a company whose sales activities are primary may find that new regulatory activity by its business sector's controlling body means that the focus on order processing has changed and more information has to be provided by law. There may be an unavoidable deadline before the new systems have to be implemented. A company's ability to be first in the field may dramatically affect its profits. An order processing system may be just the sort of system which no one expected to revolutionize the business, but which as a result of the new regulations is brought into the limelight.

For large companies, mergers and acquisitions have always caused problems for their IT departments. In some cases, the proposed amalgamation has been abandoned where the major strategic IT systems are incompatible. Outsourced IT may aggravate this as a problem. On the other hand, outsourcing can provide a solution where the information systems of a number of different subsidiary companies may all be outsourced to the same supplier, until they can be combined into one unified operation.

The procedure for bringing in changes

The change control procedure is all part of the ongoing management liaison. The contract should set out in detail: who may propose a change; any restrictions on what may be changed or at what level of seniority a change may be authorized; cost allocation in assessing and implementing the change. Through the mechanism for controlling changes, the contract balances predictability with flexibility.

Requests for changes may be put forward by either the supplier or the customer. Whatever the source of the proposal for variation, the supplier should carry out an evaluation of how long the proposed variation will take to implement; any likely costs for the customer – or any reduction in costs – and the effect on the rest of the services. In some instances this may be carried out almost immediately, for instance by noting that there will be no effect on the services, and that there will be no costs. However, an apparently trivial amendment may have many knock-on effects. A number of days should be allotted for the supplier to evaluate the impact of the proposed change on the level and standard of the services; what it would cost to implement; whether there will be any consequential savings; and to advise the customer accordingly in writing. Time limits may also be imposed for the customer to consider the supplier's evaluation and to agree the work and any associated costs.

In deciding whether the variation should be proceeded with, the customer may have no option, for instance if it is required as the result of an error, or if it is a legal imposition. There may need to be further negotiation over the speed of its introduction. The evaluation of the proposed variation will normally consist of whether it will be value for money, and what the costs and difficulties of implementation will be, in making the decision to proceed. Any change should continue to support the original objectives of the outsourcing, and indeed to benefit them. If additional staff are likely to be needed as a result of the proposed variations, the proposal may need to be discussed and senior management involved.

If it is agreed that the change should go ahead, a document usually known as a 'Change Order' should be drawn up, to set out the requirements, the costs and the time scale for the introduction. This Change Order will serve to vary formally the service level agreement or the contractual terms if necessary.

The contract should make it clear whether the evaluation process is to be without charge as part of the general services of the supplier. Depending on the method of charging, and perhaps on the nature of the proposed change, it would be typical for the supplier to accept the assessment of the change within its service provision. The return for the supplier will be in terms of the charges agreed for the work in carrying out the variation or for the extra work involved in its operation. If the supplier needs safeguards in making sure it has sufficient resources at its disposal at the time that they will be required, then a suitably worded provision in the contract for adequate notice to be given of variations, for allowance to be made for recruitment and training, and for the supplier to choose when to implement the variation, will provide protection against liability.

The change control procedure may involve a consultation process. However, there should be a requirement for the supplier to be reasonable in accepting a customer's request for variation and not to delay in proceeding with implementation. This will be important to the customer's control of its business, or where there is no option but to introduce the amendment, such as in the case of new legislation or in upgrading hardware under the terms of a lease or supply agreement.

On the other hand, it should be the customer's right to refuse to accept a variation proposed by the supplier, whether or not there is an additional cost attached. The customer has contracted for a service to be provided for which it is paying. It must have the certainty of that service at the rates agreed. An argument which may be advanced to mitigate this is that the customer should take note of the outsourcer's concern, particularly in a wholesale outsourcing. If there is disagreement because one party's requirements are considered to be unrealistic or because of a shortage of resources or budget, a dispute resolution procedure should be used and the matter escalated, as discussed in Chapter 9.

If changes are required to the terms of the contract itself rather than to the substance of the services or the service levels or the technology, the procedure should be very carefully controlled. The supplier and the customer representatives should not themselves have the powers of amending the contract. These powers should be at senior management level.

Avoiding bureaucracy

The change control procedure is important for providing a structure to the sequence, substance timing and discussion of proposed variations, so that both parties are aware of the implications. It will be necessary for the customer to know formally what the change will cost and to enable an assessment to be made of any additional costs and any effects on the rest of the outsourced systems, and when the change will take place. At the same time, the procedure must not be so bureaucratic that it will not be followed or that it will cause delay. The variation itself must always be documented and the service level agreements amended if necessary. This documentation should be kept with the contract as part of the contract administration process. It may be helpful to number the changes. They should at least be dated and retained in chronological sequence or filed according to the part of the system which is affected by the variation.

If the procedure is not followed, discussions *after* the change has been effected about who is to pay or about the delays caused by its introduction and consequences for the rest of the system can become acrimonious.

The definition of the scope of the services should be clear on what is to be regarded as part of the normal services being undertaken by the supplier. This may include some additional work which would replicate similar general assistance provided to end users by an in-house IT department. However, a problem which may arise in practice is that the supplier's staff will often willingly carry out small variations free of charge beyond what is set out in the service level agreements, in order to keep the relationship with the customer happy, and because from their point of view it seems a simple enough modification to implement. This raises the customer's expectations of what can be achieved for the price being paid. If in fact service level performance is subsequently affected, then arguments ensue. In order to discourage this, the supplier must ensure that its staff are subject to the disciplines of recording variations. The supplier should always make it clear that any work for which there is to be no charge is not part of the agreed requirements – reserving the right to charge for other work.

Thus all changes should be formally recorded and signed off as part of the change control procedures set out in the contract.

Confidentiality, Data Protection and Security

From a security perspective, an outsourcing contract should cover:

- confidentiality and integrity requirements;

- obligations relating to personal data;

- if the supplier or the customer is a public sector organization, a means for managing relevant information which may be subject to access requests under freedom of information legislation;

- the supplier's commitments in respect of security management, including compliance with standards and the requirements of rules of any relevant regulatory bodies, such as those for certain financial systems;

- contingency planning and disaster recovery.

Broad contractual statements about confidentiality and security will demonstrate the general ethos which should apply to the outsourcing activities. Nevertheless, this is no substitute for identifying the areas for which specific assurances are important, to enable the contractual commitments to be precisely expressed. This identification process will form part of the customer's risk management strategy, in reviewing how secure in practice each of the systems and kinds of information for which the services are being provided should be, relatively or absolutely.

Before negotiating the outsourcing contract, the importance of confidentiality arises at the preliminary stages of dealing with specialist consultants and prospective suppliers. This is discussed in Chapter 2.

Protecting confidential information

A customer's trade secrets and sensitive or valuable business information should be expressly protected by the contract. Whether the supplier is working day-by-day at the customer's premises, or dealing with the customer's systems and information at its own premises, it will be in a position to acquire information within the operational environment which is not for general circulation. If the supplier specialises in the area of the customer's business, it may wish to extend its knowledge of that sector for future outsourcing opportunities. What is discussed at the joint management meetings may concern future customer strategy and not be general knowledge.

Standard confidentiality clauses are likely to be taken far less seriously than unambiguous provisions on what information does need to be treated with extra care, and any special procedures which should be followed. If possible, the customer should detail the kind of information which is of concern, whether because of its substance or its form: information about the structure of the business, financial data, customer lists, whatever may be accessible to the supplier's staff. The more distinctively the provision addresses the confidentiality requirement, the better the chances of its efficacy.

The provisions may extend to requirements for the supplier to keep its staff informed of what is to be regarded as confidential, and to have special procedures for looking after the information, such as restrictions on its processing and instructions concerning its destruction. If the supplier will be using the services of third party contractors who will be entitled to access confidential information, the supplier must take responsibility in the contract for their compliance with confidentiality arrangements.

An exception should be made for disclosure of confidential information to auditors and other professional advisers or regulators.

The supplier's proprietary information

In carrying out the outsourcing work, the supplier's staff are bound to develop know-how, ideas and techniques. This expertise is less easily definable than 'confidential information'. As part of the employees' skills, this know-how will be transferable for them to use in work for other customers, either during the outsourcing if there is a downturn in the customer's requirements and the supplier is able to move some resources to more profitable contracts, or in the future, at the end of the outsourcing. The customer will not be able to prevent this.

The parties may both have legitimate reasons for wanting to keep the actual contract details confidential to the parties, since these will be so intimately connected with their respective practices and strategies. However, within any such restriction the customer must avoid any constraints on being able to pass information to third party advisers or experts, for example those whom it might wish to consult if the outsourcing services prove unsatisfactory or increase in cost unexpectedly while the contract is in force, or in its negotiations with other potential suppliers when the contract is coming to an end.

Data protection principles

The Data Protection Act, the law in the UK,[1] results from a European Commission Directive[2] that applies to member states of the European Union, which therefore should all have equivalent laws. The objective is to protect the privacy of the personal data of the data subjects, yet in so doing, to enable organizations to use such information legitimately. The law itself has been drawn up, and associated regulations and codes subsequently developed, so as to ensure that this objective may be effectively achieved.

Compliance with the Act's eight Data Protection Principles is required. These Principles are a code of practice which cover all aspects of processing personal data, so as to achieve a balance between the need for personal data to be processed and the protection of the individual's right to privacy.

There are additional criteria for holding and processing 'sensitive' personal data, for example those relating to health, ethnicity, criminal convictions, and so on. At least one of a list of conditions must be met: for instance, the subject must have given express consent, or the information must be required by law for employment purposes, or in the administration of justice.

---

1   Data Protection Act 1998.
2   Directive 95/46 EC on the protection of individuals with regard to the processing of personal data and on the free movement of such data.

Data controller and data processor

The 'data controller' is the organization which determines why and how it should be holding and processing personal data, takes decisions about the personal data, and is therefore accountable for complying with the data protection principles. A service provider which processes personal data on behalf of the data controller is defined as a 'data processor'. In an outsourcing arrangement involving personal data, the customer will be the data controller and the outsourcing provider will be the data processor.

In the relationship of data controller and data processor, legal obligations are specifically imposed on both parties so that the processing continues to be authorized and lawful, and especially for compliance with the seventh principle: 'Appropriate technical and organizational measures shall be taken against unauthorized or unlawful processing of personal data, and against accidental loss or destruction of, or damage to, personal data.'. The data controller remains responsible for the personal data, for security in particular and for compliance with the data protection principles in general. In carrying out the processing service, the data processor is responsible for data security and must be contractually accountable to the data controller.

The data controller must ensure that the data processor is suitable for providing the necessary 'technical and organizational security measures' in respect of the processing. It is a requirement for there to be a written contract with the data processor to ensure that the appropriate standards will be applied. This will be part of the outsourcing services contract, but consideration may need to be given as to whether this should be a separate agreement, incorporated into the overall contract, for the ability to reference and monitor its detail by the individuals charged with putting it into practice. As part of this agreement, the data processor must act only on instructions from the data controller in respect of the personal data and guarantee the security of the processing and the integrity of the personal data.

Transferring personal data abroad

The eighth data protection principle prohibits the transfer of personal data outside the European Economic Area (EEA)[3] unless the transferee country has an 'adequate level of protection' for the rights of the data subjects whose personal data is transferred. In this context, transfer of the personal data is from

---

3   The European Economic Area comprises the member states of the European Union together with Iceland, Norway and Liechtenstein.

the data controller – who, once the data have been transferred, will not be in a position to control its processing – to a third party controller (rather than to a data processor).

The data controller has to assess that the level of protection for the personal data is 'adequate' in all the circumstances of the place of transfer, its legal system and international obligations, and that the security measures taken are satisfactory, before authorizing the transfer.

For a number of countries the European Commission has confirmed by means of a 'Community finding' that the laws do provide an adequate level of protection: for example, for Switzerland.

The United States has a different approach to data protection from the EU, which consists of a combination of various laws and self-regulation. Agreement has been reached between the EU and the US Department of Commerce for a voluntary regime known as the 'Safe Harbor'. Those American companies which subscribe to this regime thereby agree to abide by rules which are recognized as providing adequate protection for personal data transferred from the EU. EU data exporters wishing to check whether their intended US recipient enjoys 'Safe Harbor' status (American spelling) can refer to a publicly available list maintained by the Department of Commerce.

Data transfers to US organizations outside the Safe Harbor must be covered under one of the exemptions discussed below.

EXEMPTION BY CONTRACT

Where the transfer of personal data is outside the EEA, but not to a country where there is a Community Finding or to a US company which is committed to the Safe Harbor rules, it must fall within a number of legal exemptions to be permitted. Thus one of the exemptions is that the data subject has given express informed consent for the transfer – although in an outsourcing context, this is unlikely to be typically invoked (except as part of additional requirements for processing or transfer of sensitive personal data).

Another exemption is given for a contract providing adequate express safeguards to protect the transfer of personal data, according to which the recipient in the destination country must be committed to guaranteeing sufficient protection.

In outsourcing, a written contract is required between the data controller and the data processor in respect of the processing of personal data by the data processor, whether or not the data processor is a company based in an EEA country. The contract needs to be applicable to the particular circumstances of the outsourcing in any event. There may need to be additional terms to allow for the specific situation where the data processor is outside the EEA. As such, the data processor is not directly subject to the enforceable rules of the EU on data protection, as the data controller organization is, under the laws of the jurisdiction in which it is established, but the contract is the means for enabling the requirements to be legally enforced.

Standard or model clauses approved by the European Commission and authorized by the Information Commissioner provide adequate safeguards for use, either for data controller-data controller or for data controller-data processor. These model provisions are available at the Information Commissioner's website,[4] together with guidance on use. They may be used as a stand-alone contract or incorporated into a contract between the parties. The European Commission's own form of wording for the data controller and data processor relationship refers to the data controller as the 'data exporter' and to the data processor as the 'data importer'.

However, it is not compulsory to use any specific wording. Some of the standard formats are long, detailed and legalistic, and impose high levels of liability on both parties. In the overall context of an outsourcing, clauses may be drawn up between the parties to reflect the particular agreement more accurately, which provide adequate protection for the personal information.

In any event it is important for the supplier to be a reputable company with demonstrable ability to ensure security of the personal data. It should make checks on individual members of staff for their compliance in keeping personal data secure. It should be required to report security breaches to the customer, and the customer should have procedures for dealing with any. Audits should be carried out by or on behalf of the customer from time to time.

BINDING CORPORATE RULES

Occasionally a form of outsourcing takes place between a customer in the UK and a supplier company outside the EEA which both belong within the same international group of companies. Their structures and operations may not lend themselves to transferring personal data under model contracts or with

---

4   http://www.ico.gov.uk.

the subject's consent. In these circumstances, a mechanism known as 'binding corporate rules' may enable the personal data to be transferred between the companies.

Under these rules, each company within the group agrees to conform with an internal corporate-wide code of conduct for international transfers of personal data within the group of companies. The procedure must include the substantive data protection requirements, legal enforceability by data subjects, training, audit and complaint handling. It must be demonstrable that the rules are known and understood. The procedure must be binding in practice and legally. A single national data protection supervisory authority – normally in the place where the organization has its European headquarters – must approve the procedure as adequate on behalf of the national data protection authorities in all the EU member states involved. A model checklist and procedure for a set of corporate rules has been adopted to use in making an application to the relevant data protection authority for approval, and is available at the Information Commissioner's website.[5]

But legal enforceability within a group of companies is problematic. The effectiveness of this mechanism is dependent on a high standard of good corporate governance within the group of companies, on the ability to require compliance from an individual company, and on sanctions which would be legally enforceable.

Freedom of information access

Any member of the public has a general right of access by written request to recorded information held by about 100,000 public sector organizations under freedom of information laws.[6] These organizations include government departments; local and health authorities; governing bodies of maintained schools and further and higher educational institutions; advisory committees, Boards and Commissions, ranging from the Adjudicator for the Inland Revenue and Customs and Excise to the Zoos Forum.

For the outsourcing business environment, not only public sector customers are affected, but also any suppliers working with public sector organizations, who provide information in bidding for the work, or during the outsourcing, and in their contracts and contract performance – implementation plans,

---

5   http://www.dataprotection.gov.uk.
6   Freedom of Information Act 2000; Freedom of Information (Scotland) Act 2002.

service levels, ongoing commercial discussions. This information is potentially disclosable. The law is retrospective – previous contracts are also subject to access.

There is no right of access to information which is designated by the Act as absolutely exempt, such as information about national security, defence and law enforcement – not unexpectedly. Exemptions likely to apply commercially are information which is provided in confidence and (separately) trade secrets and information likely to prejudice commercial interests. These categories are narrower in operation than might be apparent.

Information provided in confidence is exempt from disclosure by the public authority if disclosure would constitute an actionable breach of confidence at law. This is very restricted. Under other circumstances, this is one of the reasons for recommending non-disclosure agreements, because confidential information is not guaranteed to be legally protected simply by being described as such. The information must have the 'necessary quality of confidence', be imparted in circumstances where it is obvious that there must be an obligation of confidence, and communication of that information be to the detriment of the person who originally imparted it. These vague criteria provide much scope for argument over the uncertainty of what constitutes information provided in confidence.

Trade secrets and information likely to prejudice commercial interests – of the public authority holding the information or those of a third party – are a 'qualified exemption'. A 'trade secret' is also very narrowly interpreted, on criteria such as the extent of skill, effort or innovation required to create it, the amount invested in developing the information, the efforts made to guard its secrecy, and so on.

Such information is not automatically exempt, and merely stating that it falls within the exemptions is not enough. It must also be in the public interest that the information is not divulged – and the authority must document the reason for a refusal to do so, for example that there is a substantial risk of prejudice to business by giving commercial advantage to competitors, or that it would cause loss of shareholder or customer confidence. Moreover, the situation may change over time – information may become less commercially sensitive or the balance of public interest may shift.

The Secretary of State for Constitutional Affairs' Code of Practice reviews statutory prohibitions on the disclosure of information and gives guidance about exemptions.[7] Amongst other things it advises public authorities to reject 'contractual terms which purport to restrict the disclosure of information', or confidentiality clauses relating to the terms of the contract, its value and performance. It is the public authority's legal responsibility to determine if an exemption applies, in responding to a request. It should not be willing simply to accept information in confidence. The characteristic of 'confidentiality' must be justified, and the information given only if it is necessary for the exercise of the authority's functions and would not otherwise be provided.

Withholding information from the person requesting it may be acceptable where disclosure would discourage future provision of commercially sensitive information and undermine the public authority's ability to function, or where disclosure would affect its negotiating ability, or where other transactions with public authorities would be inhibited. When a decision is taken to withhold information, an audit trail should be created to show how the decision was reached and the reasons for the refusal. Information will be disclosed where it demonstrates transparency and accountability in the use of public funds, shows that there is value for money and that commercial activities are conducted openly.

The Office for Government Commerce, OGC,[8] provides some model clauses for contracts between contractors and public authorities to deal with 'commercially sensitive information' and 'confidential information'. These clauses require the contractor to be extremely careful when disclosing the information, and emphasize that the public sector customer will still have to consider the applicability of the exemption on a case-by-case basis and comply with the Code of Practice. These clauses are drafted in favour of the public sector party and should certainly not be adopted wholesale without considering whether they will actually be helpful to the parties in the particular circumstances. They are certainly no guarantee for the private contractor against disclosure.

A public authority is not required to keep a third party informed if considering releasing information about a company. If the information is not sensitive – under the public authority's criteria – it can be released without consultation. If it may be sensitive, then the company should be consulted, but it is finally the authority's decision. Nevertheless, it is good practice for a public authority to give notice to a third party if it proposes to disclose information

---

7   http://www.justice.gov.uk/guidance/foi-code-of-practice.htm.
8   http://www.ogc.gov.uk.

relating to that third party, or at least draw attention to the disclosure once made.

Both parties should review existing contracts, as the confidentiality provisions in some of these contracts may no longer be applicable for either party.

Private sector companies can help themselves in attempting to prevent disclosure. They must continually review the information they supply to public authorities, on a case-by-case basis. They must understand that information in the possession of the public authority will be disclosed if a request for disclosure is made – which could be by a journalist or a competitor – and it is regarded as in the public interest to do so.

Suppliers' standard terms and conditions for public authorities need to be amended to cover freedom of information requirements. General confidentiality provisions will not be sufficient. Suppliers will need to agree specific clauses which will be enforceable, at the outset of communicating with any public authority. From the moment that communication with public authorities starts, that is to say from the time when the contractors may be providing information which may be disclosable, they should ensure by means of contract that they will be notified promptly of any request for information relating to them and be consulted about its release. This gives them the chance of persuading the public authority that it is not in fact in the public interest that the information concerned should be disclosed. If the persuasion is unsuccessful, there is at least a short time to work on damage limitation.

Commercially sensitive information that is handed over should be so structured and presented that it is separable from other information, for example in its own self-contained schedule, and that it can therefore be redacted. Its eventual demise should be specified, a time limit when it must be returned, destroyed or archived.

There is very little that private companies can do in practice to prevent disclosure, and once disclosure has happened, it is too late to remedy the situation in any effective way.

These are defensive recommendations for companies' risk management of their own information. Conversely, it is worth considering if there is information held by public authorities about their own processes or about competitors that it would be useful for a company to obtain legitimately in order to achieve strategic benefits and competitive advantage in any way.

Security

The range of threats affecting organizations may be internal or external, including accidents, malicious actions and industrial sabotage.

The DTI Information Security Breaches Survey 2004[9] says:

> *'The number of businesses that suffered a security breach continues to rise ... two-thirds of UK businesses had a premeditated or malicious incident ... a quarter had a significant incident involving accidental systems failure or data corruption. The average UK business now has roughly one security breach a month. Large businesses have roughly one a week.'*

This costs the businesses concerned serious money.

Access to computer systems must always be properly authorized. This may be by means of a general authorization for the supplier in the contract. Any third party contractors who need to access the systems should be given authorization entitlements within their consultancy service contracts with the supplier, in exchange for specific confidentiality obligations. Additionally there may be systems of password access, and reinforcement of what is permitted by means of notices indicating copyright and stating that only permitted users have the right of access to the systems, which appear on screen at the time when the password is requested.

The customer's data must be kept secure, with regular back up procedures, and appropriate levels of authorization set for those supplier's staff entitled to access, preocess and use the data. There should be an audit trail. Any requirements for the supplier to manage security specifically, for example in respect of staff, data, disaster recovery, equipment, premises, or compliance with standards, must be built into the service level agreements and be legally enforceable. These provisions will encompass regular day-to-day security requirements.

A high proportion of service level agreements do contain information security standard requirements, mostly for compliance with the customer's

---

9   http://www.infosec.co.uk/files/DTI_Survey_Report.pdf.

own security rules. This means that they need to be properly defined. The contract may require the supplier to comply with external security standards, such as to have certification for information security management.

The ISO 27000 series consists of international standards for information security management. The International Organization for Standardization, 'ISO', is a non-governmental organization, a network of national standards institutes of over 150 countries, co-ordinated by a Central Secretariat in Geneva.[10] ISO 27000 comprises the terminology, the vocabulary and definitions.[11] ISO 27001 consists of the information systems management requirements standard/specification against which organizations are certified. Its objective is to 'provide a model for establishing, implementing, operating, monitoring, reviewing, maintaining, and improving an Information Security Management System' within the context of the organization's overall business risks. ISO 27002 used to be ISO 17799, formerly the BS 7799 Part 1 standard: a Code of Practice describing a set of information security management objectives and controls. These standards are widely used; for example they are recommended practice in the NHS Connecting for Health programme.

They provide a basis for best practice in developing, implementing and measuring effective information security management.

If the customer's security is governed by regulatory requirements of its sector, then it must obtain specific commitments from the supplier. Thus financial services businesses are regulated in many jurisdictions by local regulators. In the UK, it is the Financial Services Authority (FSA), which is a non-governmental body established by the Financial Services and Markets Act 2000.[12] This Act has set objectives, which include maintaining confidence in financial systems; protecting consumers; and reducing financial crime. The FSA provides guidance on outsourcing for those firms which it regulates.

Contingency planning and disaster recovery

The outsourcing services should include documented contingency planning, and third party disaster recovery procedures if appropriate, to enable normal services to be restored as soon as possible in the event of exceptional problems.

---

10 http://www.iso.org/iso/home.htm.
11 http://www.27000.org.
12 http://www.fsa.gov.uk.

If contingency plans already exist for the customer's information systems functions, these must be reviewed for their adequacy in an outsourcing situation. It is frequently the case, however, that the customer has not previously given serious attention to the possibility of one-off catastrophes which could affect its systems capability. The process of deciding what procedures would be necessary and how they should be implemented would therefore need to be initiated as part of the contract preparations, ideally hand-in-hand with ascertaining the standards for the service levels.

Different degrees of back up will be necessary, according to the importance of the particular system or data to the customer, to the priorities assessed by the customer, and on the length of time a system can be out of action without affecting the customer's business. For some systems, the result will be inconvenience only. For others, for example where real time processing affects business decisions, recovery must be immediate.

In the event of physical disaster striking the machines or the premises where the IT services are carried out, the supplier may be able to provide its own disaster recovery systems for critical systems at alternative sites of its own, or a separate disaster recovery contract may be agreed with a third party for temporary processing at a remote site. The manufacturer concerned may be able to help with schemes for replacement hardware. It may be that the services are provided at a number of customer sites, and that there can be reciprocal fallback arrangements at a site which is unaffected by a disaster.

The contingency plan should therefore cover action plans for recovery to normal conditions following a disaster, once the extent of the damage has been assessed and actions prioritized depending on the relative criticality of the systems to the business. Provision for the supplier to test the contingency plan from time to time should be built in.

It should be set out in terms agreed by both the supplier and the customer, and incorporated into the contract. The supplier should then be able to give contractual assurances that the outsourcing services could be continued through any circumstances preventing normal operation, particularly for critical systems or services.

In considering the extent of security levels which are necessary, it should be borne in mind that the more rigorous the security procedures and record keeping that are demanded, the higher the costs for the customer will be.

Contract Duration, Termination and Transition Management

Outsourcing must be a finite arrangement, not an open-ended commitment. The decision on how long the contract should last is an important one. The contract will eventually expire if not terminated earlier. At this time the customer has the choice of inviting renewal if the outsourcing supplier is willing to carry on providing the services, whether by re-negotiation or on the existing basis, or seeking further tenders or bringing the work back in-house.

Whatever the outcome, continuity of the services must be ensured through contractual commitments, and at all costs avoiding total dependence by the customer on the supplier – 'lock in'. There must be safeguards built in to the contract so that the customer will never be left stranded at the point of no return, even in the event of breach or disagreement.

Towards the end of the term, if the customer is comparing new bids for the work, the supplier will be expected to make relevant information available about the services. If the outcome is that a different supplier or an in-house team is to take over the outsourcing, the handover by the supplier must include everything necessary for the service provision to be carried on, and the situation in respect of staff, equipment and software licences must be controlled.

Grounds on which the services may exceptionally be terminated early should be identified in the contract.

Looking ahead to the end

Most of the contract negotiations will be concerned with putting the framework in place, the transfer and management of resources and assets, the levels of service and the day-to-day operational practices once handover has occurred.

However, an outsourcing relationship is not a static affair, and is part of a larger environment that itself is subject to change which may be subtle but will certainly be constant. During the course of the contract, the customer's business practices may be modified and its focus may consequently shift. Meanwhile the supplier may be developing different strategies for gaining new work from its existing customers or it may acquire new customers whom it finds more interesting for various reasons. Personnel on both sides will move on and be replaced. It is unsafe to assume permanence or predictability either in the relationship or in the services, and the duration of the contract will therefore almost inevitably be for a fixed term.

How long should the contract last?

A small self-contained system or an obsolescent function may conveniently be outsourced for a short period, such as three to five years. The outsourcing of the whole IT function of a major company will more typically be for an initial term of longer than this, with options to continue, and ongoing scope for variation.

Where the contract term is relatively short, charging rates may be linked to its duration, giving some certainty of income and expenditure for the supplier and customer respectively. The first increase in charges may then be imposed at the time when the contract term is due to be extended.

The climate of business uncertainty, increasing regulatory issues and growing awareness of supplier leverage are two factors contributing to caution in deciding the length of the term. For selective outsourcing, this is also realistic. Built-in renewal provisions will enable the parties to continue the relationship if it is working effectively. But how far is it reasonable for a company to look ahead in this environment? How far forward does its business plan extend? How realistically can any organization assess the numbers of people to be employed in the forthcoming years? What new technologies will be utilized? For instance, email and use of the internet have been widely adopted only in the last decade. Evidence also tends to show that it is the contracts of longer than five years which are likely to cause problems.

Nevertheless, ten- or twelve-year terms or longer are often negotiated, especially for public sector profit sharing contracts, and especially for business transformation outsourcing. For example, Pearl Assurance Group was reported as outsourcing all its operational systems for a twelve-year term to the UK company, Diligenta, of an Indian supplier, TCS. TCS took a lease of a building, took over staff, committed to fixed prices and to building a centre of excellence of the administration of life assurance and pensions. The rationale was for a strategy to allow for declining business in the closed life insurance funding sector, managing the regulatory risk side, and transforming the information systems – at a better price, with staff career options. Pearl Assurance believed that it would be difficult for an outsourcer to achieve these purposes without enough time to do so.[1]

Checks and checkpoints

For contracts of long duration, a structure of formal checkpoints should be in place to review that the outsourcing is working consistently throughout the term, to build in scope for variations in the charges and to the services, and to set points at which negotiations may be re-opened for particular aspects.

Benchmarking is one good formal way of reviewing the contract at set times whilst it is in force. The prevailing market prices of a group of services may be compared at regular intervals with the prices being charged under the contract, taking into account new technologies which may cut costs. The contract should allow for charges to be re-negotiated if prices have fallen due to new technologies which should properly be taken into account, or for other reasons. This is discussed further in Chapter 8.

For an extensive and complex outsourcing, the customer will sometimes feel more secure by instigating an initial transfer term of some months prior to a cut-over date, on the principle that if the supplier is not performing in that time as anticipated and agreed, the customer will then be able to terminate early without having to pay any compensation to the supplier. There may be other reasons when a short transfer period may appear to be desirable: perhaps for administrative purposes to finalise the leases and asset transfers, or for working out service level details. But if it is not an intrinsic part of the transaction structure, a bedding-in trial period is likely to do no more than to provide a perceived psychological benefit for the team or director ultimately responsible for negotiating the contract for the customer. If problems were to be encountered in practice in these first months of a large-scale contract, where so much energy had been expended in choosing the supplier and drawing up the contract, the whole worth of the extensive process of selection and negotiation would be open to question. The customer would look indecisive. The supplier would be having to give business assurances in a wholly unsatisfactory atmosphere of uncertainty which would not be conducive to long term planning and a positive mutual understanding.

---

1   Reported in *Computing*, 12 October 2006, page 46.

Another possibility is to set phases for the contract. For example, Swansea City Council signed a ten-year contract with Capgemini in 2006 after eighteen months delay in negotiations caused by strike action by its own staff. In Phase 1 systems were to be replaced and IT support provided. Phase 2 was to introduce a new call centre, face-to-face contact centre, 24x7 online services and a single point of contact for customers. Shortly afterwards it was decided to cancel Phase 2 as the Council sought costs savings. But the first phase was still able to proceed. This was widely reported in the computer press.[2]

Another alternative occasionally sought by the customer is for an entitlement to early termination in spite of the fixed term. It would be necessary to build in compensation for the supplier in such an event. On the basis that the supplier will be able to re-allocate resources profitably elsewhere, the compensation will be payable only for the disruption attendant on the re-allocation and for unrecoverable capital expenditure. However, the supplier may negotiate a more substantial payment if it has planned its resources' availability for the original term, and is looking to cover its loss of profits.

On the other hand there are a number of cases where it is the supplier who has been able to negotiate an early exit, where for various reasons the contract was not providing the anticipated profits or there were greater difficulties than expected in delivering the services.

Expiry, renewal or notice

A set period for the outsourcing may be stipulated, at the end of which the contract will simply expire. This would be normal for a long-term contract. There may be provisions for the supplier to give early notice of its wish to renew, the terms on which it would do so and how the customer should respond. For less complex selective outsourcing contracts of shorter duration, there may be an automatic extension beyond the expiry date, perhaps on rolling terms of twelve months or three years, unless one party notifies the other of intention to terminate.

There are three choices for the customer when the contract is drawing to a close, any of which may be more or less realistic according to the circumstances: to stay with the supplier on either the same or re-negotiated terms; to choose another supplier, preferably by going out to tender – as part of the selection

---

2   For example, in http://www.mycustomer.com/cgi-bin/item.cgi?id=132737.

process, the current supplier may be asked to re-tender; or to bring back the work in-house.

It is important for the customer to keep in mind the date when the contract will expire and to plan for that time. It is easy to be caught out and to have to extend the term by default, not having prepared for a formal decision on whether to continue the relationship, renegotiate or set up internally.

The more complex the range of services, the more difficult it is to set up ways and means of ensuring a smooth transition to another supplier or back into the customer's organization. And the customer who is seeking to re-tender the services will have different requirements of the supplier at the end of the outsourcing contract from what will be necessary if it is bringing back the services in-house. To some extent some needs can be identified only in a general way with catch-all wording. These are nevertheless likely outcomes to prepare for. Surveys consistently show that a significant minority, around 25 per cent, of outsourced organizations end contracts with their current supplier rather than renew them.

There are at least three factors concerned in the trend towards changing supplier. New and evolving technologies, such as systems automation, benefit the economics of large scale management, with technical differentiation. Standardization of various technologies enables customers to shop around for other suppliers to support their requirements. And offshoring costs can look attractive. Nevertheless, moving an outsourcing service that is failing or coming to an end from one outsourcing supplier to another will not necessarily solve a problem or automatically reduce costs, and introduces a new level of risk.

It is also not unusual for work to be brought back in-house. Some customers become so unhappy with their outsourcing supplier that they are prepared to pay to get out of the contract before its expiry, in order to rebuild their in-house capability. Although it may seem at the outset of the contract that the whole purpose of outsourcing would be lost if it were necessary to visualize reconstituting the structure in-house again at some future point in time, this is in fact not unlikely as a future scenario, not always at the behest of the customer.

Although negotiations for renewal would normally begin well in advance of the date by which notice must be given, the notice period should be long enough for decisions to be taken about the future without unreasonable pressures. The customer needs time to re-negotiate the contract terms and conditions, perhaps to organize a re-tendering process if the services are to continue to be outsourced, possibly to find a different supplier and transfer the services, or to arrange to bring the services back in-house. The supplier needs time to seek other sources of work if its services are likely to be terminated. A re-tendering process should begin at least twelve months before expiry of the existing contract, and therefore the notice period needs to relate to this. The customer must be alert to the date for formally giving notice. Good contract administration procedures together with proper management liaison and reporting structures, as discussed in Chapter 9, will assist the customer to keep control of the timetable.

The customer may reserve a right in the contract to call for an independent audit at its own expense at the point of giving notice, the supplier agreeing to provide without charge any information reasonably needed by the auditor. The aim of this exercise would be to establish objectively the levels of service being attained in relation to the charges, at this point in the contract life, for the purpose of comparing them against the original specification of services and service levels, in order to assess the value being obtained. This may be used as a rationale for staying with the supplier on similar or re-negotiated terms, or as a basis for getting competitive quotes from third party suppliers.

The supplier's continuing commitment

Towards the end of the contract term, the future relationship between supplier and customer will appear uncertain. The customer may be looking around at other outsourcing suppliers and requesting tenders, the current supplier being offered the opportunity to put in its own bid at the same time. Yet at this time the supplier will be in control of most of the information and know-how which would be critical to any other bidder. The customer's systems may have become integrated with the provider's systems; the customer's former staff may have joined the provider's payroll; the customer may be dependent on the provider's procedures.

The supplier should undertake in the contract to provide to the customer – or to the customer's representative if the customer is using the services of outsourcing consultants – the appropriate documentation, such as procedures, guides, third party contracts and any additional information necessary to enable an effective re-tendering exercise to be carried out. This will enable potential bidders to be in a position to quote charges which have taken all the relevant information into account. The supplier should be ready and willing to help positively and constructively in providing assistance to the customer on matters relating to the services in the event of termination – even when its competitors will be involved – to do its best towards a smooth service migration. The contractual commitment will have to be of a general nature. At the time the agreement is being negotiated, it will not be clear precisely what assistance will be helpful, nor for how long it will be needed. Any requirements which are clear from the start can be contractually specified, such as retrieval or access of data in a suitable format, and the continued operation of software, and general handing back or handing over. The client will have to negotiate under time pressures to access the information to which it should be entitled, when it will not normally be in a strong position. The supplier may justifiably wish to charge for this, and the basis and rates should be agreed for including in the contract.

The beginning of the relationship is the point at which the supplier should be at its most confident and optimistic about the ongoing quality of its services, and when the termination provisions can therefore most easily be negotiated. There are no prospects of success in attempting to lay down principles of co-operation once the services have deteriorated, or the relationship has broken down, or the customer has found a more compatible supplier.

As a safeguard, the customer may find it worth negotiating to allow for the services to be carried out on the same terms or on reasonable charges for a number of months beyond the date of termination, at its option. This is effectively a limited continuation of the contract, to which the supplier may not have any objection – unless it is itself about to enter into a more lucrative contract with another party.

The supplier must continue to respect the security and confidentiality entitlements of the customer after termination and equally the customer must continue to keep secret the supplier's confidential information about its business and proprietary methodologies.

Unless the supplier finds itself in the unhappy situation of wanting to extricate itself from the relationship – for example if the services are being provided less profitably than it had calculated, or the work is not as interesting as it had hoped, or the systems are not expanding through further development as it had anticipated – the period prior to termination will be a difficult time. The effects of termination for a supplier who does not immediately have other sources of work will be severe, consisting of loss of profits and unemployed resources.

Continuity of human resources and use of assets

The TUPE Regulations[3] discussed in Chapter 6 will also apply on termination of the outsourcing contract, if the contractor loses the contract to a competitor or the services revert in-house, provided that there is a stable economic entity as described earlier, and the exclusions do not apply. There may be a sequence of outsourcing arrangements. As Peter Skyte, then national officer of the Amicus union, said:

> 'We're now dealing with people who have been outsourced and then onsourced three or four times in ten years'.[4]

Thus the contract should entitle the transferor to be given information about the transferee's staff at the termination or expiry of the contract, in the same way as on entering into the outsourcing contract, as much as is necessary for the invitation to tender for submission of bids for the next outsourcing contract, in case the Regulations will apply to the transfer of staff to another different contractor. The transferee should warrant the accuracy of the information. The transferor and any successor contractor must be protected by indemnities from the transferee in relation to employment liabilities during the term of the outsourcing, and concerning the consultation process. Staff will also need to be informed as part of the TUPE process.

If the services are not brought back in-house at the conclusion of the outsourcing contract, the original customer transferor will seek indemnities which will benefit its new supplier outsourcing relationship, so that the new supplier can cost the services realistically.

Where contracts are renewed or renegotiated but none of the staff originally involved is still around, the loss of corporate memory can become a serious problem. This can be more acute if the outsourcing has involved application systems, especially core systems and project management, rather than mainframe processing or operational networks.

The customer may consider negotiating a contractual right to approach the supplier's key staff or experienced personnel working on the contract, in particular any of the customer's former staff who had originally been transferred to the supplier, to provide continuity. (This would be an exception to any restraints which might be included in the contract on actively canvassing staff, as discussed at Chapter 6.) How far this could be successful in practice is another

---

3   Transfer of Undertakings (Protection of Employment) Regulations 2006.
4   *Computer Weekly,* 4 October 2005.

question. It would be entirely a matter for the individual personnel concerned. They cannot be forced to move or to return to a former employer, simply because they suddenly find themselves in the position of being a desirable resource in the short term on account of their knowledge and experience. Moreover, it is likely that during the contract term at least some of the transferees will have been promoted to gain wider experience as part of a career structure within the outsourcing company or will have resigned to follow their own inclinations, no longer working on the outsourcing services for their former employer.

All associated contracts, leases and licences must be investigated at termination for transfer. This may be for real property such as dedicated data centres or network management centres; for tangible assets such as equipment; and for software and other resources. The transfer may be by assignment or novation of ownership, in the same way as at the commencement of outsourcing, or re-licensing. A procedure should have been agreed in advance for recovering or repurchasing appropriate hardware, with a formula for ascertaining the purchase price, for instance net book value or fair market value.

Licences for third party software may need to be re-assigned or novated. Where the supplier has used its own proprietary software in the service provision, and it cannot easily be replaced, on termination of the contract between the supplier and the customer a licence for its use must be made available to the customer or to the new outsourcing supplier, or the source code acquired. This too is a matter for negotiation by looking ahead. The customer cannot afford the use of the supplier's own software as indispensable to the service provision if its unable to use that software after the end of the contract.

Exit management plan

A provision should be included in the contract for a plan to be drawn up for termination, a transition plan or 'exit management' plan, mainly in the customer's interests, as a programme and check list for what to do, and what to hand over, as the contract draws to its close. The plan will cover all the activities needed in the transfer of the services from the supplier so that their migration back to the customer in-house or to another supplier can be carried out as seamlessly as possible in an atmosphere which may well be tense.

At best the provisions should be applicable for whatever the circumstances of termination are. It may be appropriate to have a different alternative plan if there is a fault-based reason for one party to terminate. This may be very difficult to draw up initially, but should at least be considered.

The plan may include the following:

- a list of processes for managing the transition;

- the job titles of those vested with authority for dealing with the various elements;

- the resources which will be called on;

- plans for TUPE application if relevant;

- a plan for communicating with staff of both parties, and with third party suppliers and customers;

- provision of operational information;

- continuation of data delivery;

- an outline programme for transfers, assignments or novations of assets, licences of intellectual property rights and any other contracts relating to the provision of services;

- consideration of know how transfer and continuity to the extent this is possible;

- allocation of responsibilities and charges for transition services, and their basis;

- rules for access by the customer to employees and contractors;

- flexibility commitments over the transition;

- programme for transition;

- if assets were transferred to the supplier, or acquired to use for the outsourcing during the course of the contract, the plan should cover what is to happen on termination, whether the value will have been written down, or whether they should be transferred back to the customer or on to the new supplier.

A number of provisions must be included in the contract itself as individual contractual commitments if decisions are taken early, but it is also useful to have a comprehensive list of activities and processes noted in one place in the exit management plan, which should be incorporated into the contract.

The transition tasks should be kept independent of the normal service delivery process to avoid any danger of the service provision being compromised.

It is a matter for negotiation as to who should prepare the exit management plan, and at whose cost. It may be offered by the supplier as part of the overall services, and agreed by the customer. Ideally it should be drawn up before the contract comes into effect, but this is a counsel of perfection and it is more realistic to set a fixed period in the contract, such as 120 days from the date the contract commences, for it to be compiled and agreed.

It should be recognized that any exit management plan drafted at an early stage of the contract relationship is going to be in outline form and incomplete. It is in the customer's interests in a long term arrangement to keep the plan up-to-date and it should certainly be formally reviewed from time to time, with formal arrangements for doing this set out in the contract. The customer may require a review of the adequacy and currency of the plan to be included in its internal audit regime.

Reasons for early termination

The right to early termination before the contract has run its full course may be caused by breakdown of the relationship following breach of contract, or by either party's change of status, insolvency or imminent insolvency. The risk of the supplier's financial instability may be limited by such devices as escrow arrangements (discussed in Chapter 7), or guarantees from parent companies. It would be practical for the customer to get to know those individuals familiar with the services who would need employment if the employer organization ceased to exist.

The customer may terminate for breach of contract, because of the number or seriousness of breaches of service levels by the supplier, or by reason of fundamental financial, technical or organizational problems in the provision of the services. The supplier will require the ability to terminate if there are continuing problems over payment by the customer, or difficulties preventing it being able to carry out the services.

If the management procedures are working effectively, any problem should first be dealt with through the contractual escalation procedure of different levels of liaison. The termination provision will be invoked only if the escalation procedures do not produce effective results.

Early termination is not a right to exercise lightly. It will cause all sorts of problems for both parties, but it may be calculated to be the lesser evil where the alternative is to let an inadequate service continue. The customer always has to balance the costs in terms of the acceptance of disappointing services against the costs of terminating through breach on this account. This is an intrinsic difficulty in termination. Bringing in another service provider meanwhile would not only be expensive – for whichever party would eventually be responsible for the costs as between a deficient supplier and an aggrieved customer – but would not in the short term be practicable without considerable disruption. There would be the expense of temporary contract staff, together with the extra efforts which would have to be made by senior management.

A provision may be included to give either party the opportunity of making amends before the final drastic right of termination is invoked. It would be reasonable to allow a period of grace, say thirty days, to give the supplier a final chance of improving its performance. Similarly, before the supplier terminates for non-payment, the customer should be advised that if payment has not been received within a number of days, termination would be the consequence. Negotiation should be carried out with the customer's objective in sight, and it may be that payment of a reasonable sum to the supplier for (say) transfer of data and continued licensing of the software, may enable the relationship to decline in a more co-operative manner.

The contractual right to terminate for breach of contract may be limited to 'material' or 'substantial' breach, to avoid the contract being ended precipitously. The customer may exercise this right if the supplier is not meeting its contractual obligations – where the service is consistently not being carried out effectively so that service levels are not being met or there is other negligence such that internal remedies and escalation procedures will not work.

On termination by giving contractual notice there is no intrinsic obligation for reasons to be given. But where termination is on grounds of breach of contract, a dispute is almost inevitable, and the reason being given is likely to be challenged.

The customer should ensure that terms are included in the contract to require the services to be continued by the supplier in the event of disagreement. The supplier must not have the contractual right to suspend or withdraw services if there is conflict. The supplier may be prepared to agree to continue to provide the services if the customer is willing to make its normal payments into a third party stakeholder account, rather than by not paying and being in breach itself.

When there is so much effort being invested in choosing a satisfactory supplier, and in agreeing the service levels and other terms of the contract, it can be difficult for the customer to remember that the association with the supplier is bound not to be permanent. Yet it is essential to articulate the exit routes clearly at the time the contract is being negotiated, when a dispassionate view can be taken by both parties on the ways of bringing the contract to an end, the related procedures planned and the details elaborated.

Redressing Fault and Failure

CHAPTER 13

In addition to setting out the functions and responsibilities of the parties, the outsourcing contract will state the level of commercial and legal risk accepted by each party in the transaction. How much risk can each party afford to bear?

At the time of drawing up and negotiating the contract, the problems that might arise in the operation of the outsourcing services should be envisaged. The mechanisms for controlling them will be elaborated and agreed. During negotiations, a priority is to find ways of avoiding and minimising risk as far as possible, of allocating risk between the parties, and of managing risk in operating the contract. There must be adequate control techniques in place to enable the customer to maintain at least the basic services in the event of the supplier's failure or delay, or on termination of the contract. Following this, agreement must be reached as to what limits of liability are acceptable.

Some risks will legitimately be excluded under the contract. For example, the supplier may exclude any liability for failing to meet the time laid down for production of a report, where this depends upon input from end users which did not arrive by the stipulated deadline. Other contractual provisions will govern the extent to which liability will be acceptable, such as a financial limit dictated by the supplier's insurance cover. At law however, the parties are not free to contract wholly on their own terms, or entirely on those of the more powerful party, in respect of limiting or excluding liability.

What happens if anything does go wrong? Continuing failure by the supplier to meet service levels or failure by the customer to make payments at the agreed times are examples of breaches of obligations in the contract. Administrative procedures for monitoring the contract will help to control the risks. Failure to meet the critical service levels may lead to pre-agreed compensation payments. The innocent party will attempt to enforce the contract. If the dispute cannot be averted, it must be resolved. If escalating management procedures and informal negotiation processes do not succeed, there may have to be recourse to formal adjudication.

The party at fault will be liable for damage suffered by the other party, to the extent agreed in the contract, or as settled through negotiation, or decided by the courts or other means of dispute resolution.

> 'Retrieving a contract that goes wrong is more expensive and difficult than you would imagine; this is true even when there are termination clauses in place in the original contract.'[1]

This statement was made several years ago, but is still valid.

What can go wrong for the customer?

The customer will try to protect itself against the risks that the services contracted for will not be provided adequately, and that the supplier's performance is less good than had been anticipated.

Throughout the chapters of this book, individual risks in outsourcing for the customer are discussed from the perspective of avoiding the risk or limiting the damage by means of the contract. The principal risks include hidden costs or escalating costs; loss of control by the customer over its strategic use of IT; the supplier's confident claims of competence when bidding for the work not being fulfilled in practice; performance which deteriorates over time; lock-in to the contract.

When performance has sharply or consistently worsened, the difficulty in practice for the customer is to know at what stage to take the decision to end the relationship and terminate the contract. The business must be kept running and there must be provisions in the agreement to facilitate this. It is not in the customer's interests to rush to legal proceedings as soon as a problem arises, yet there may come a point when the contract has to be enforced.

What can go wrong for the supplier?

The fear of risk is not all one-sided. Suppliers are in the commercial business of outsourcing, and must ensure that payment is commensurate with what is

---

1   Willcocks and Fitzgerald, *A Business Guide to Outsourcing IT*, Business Intelligence Limited, 1994.

being offered and with making a reasonable profit. Mechanisms for payment will be included in the contract for the supplier's benefit. If there is any genuine difficulty or extended delay on the part of the customer in meeting the payment, the supplier must have the right to suspend or terminate the contract.

Beyond these requirements the supplier will use the agreement to limit its liability arising from work contractually undertaken to a reasonable extent compatible with the scope and nature of the work.

The supplier's view of risk allocation is to ensure that it will not be held responsible for any faults which it has not caused. Actions, delays or omissions by end users or other contractors or the customer itself may have led to the problem. The customer may argue that the risk belongs to the business to which the supplier is providing services. On this interpretation there is no reason why the consequences of failure of another contractor should not be borne as much by the supplier as by the customer. The customer will expect only one party to take responsibility, not to have the possibility of different parties denying liability by blaming each other.

Failure without fault

Not all deficiencies in the performance of a contract will be attributable to the fault of one or both of the parties. Historically in law it used to be the case that if a promise were to be made in a contract, then it absolutely bound the party making it, however the circumstances surrounding the performance of the contract might change. Over time, case law developed from this uncompromising position, to permit the contract to be brought to an end without blame attaching to either party, if it became impossible for the contractual obligations to be performed. The contract is said to be 'frustrated'. All sums paid will be recoverable and no further sums will fall due.

However, this applies only within very narrow limits, to an unforeseen supervening event fundamentally related to the objective of the contract beyond the control of the parties, creating a situation radically different from the original expectations. For example, the contract would be frustrated if its whole purpose was for something to be done which was subsequently prohibited by an Act of Parliament changing the law, *before* the purpose was effected. An old case on this concerned a contract for the construction of a reservoir, for completion within six years. After the First World War began, the Government ordered the contractor to stop work because the workers and the equipment were needed for the war. No one had foreseen this when the contract had been made. No one knew how long the war would last, and it would have been illegal to continue the work. The contract for building the reservoir was therefore frustrated.[2]

Causes beyond the reasonable control of either of the parties which prevent performance once the contract is in force, such as freak weather conditions or terrorist activities, are referred to as *force majeure*. Delay or failure in carrying out the contractual obligations because of force majeure reasons will not constitute legal frustration. To protect a party from being liable on the occurrence of these kinds of causes, a provision is found in many contracts which suspends the contract during the force majeure conditions. To allow some certainty to be imposed on an unsatisfactory situation, the provision may give either party the right to terminate if the situation continues for a defined period of time, perhaps 90 days.

A force majeure clause gives both parties the confidence that they can abandon the contractual requirements if either of them is constrained by events over which it is powerless. For so long as performance is suspended for the force majeure reasons, the party unable to carry out its obligations will not be in breach.

It may be helpful for the wording of the clause to specify causes which, left unstated, could involve arguments over whether they should genuinely fall under the force majeure umbrella. Industrial action affecting either party may or may not be regarded as justifying non-performance; fundamental damage to hardware, however caused, may be considered in a similar light.

The clause is often inserted automatically in many kinds of contracts. Nevertheless, for an outsourcing contract which includes disaster recovery provisions, and where reliance is being placed on the delivery of a service within highly constrained parameters, a customer should reflect on whether any failure by the supplier to perform could ever be regarded as reasonable, especially if there are comprehensive contingency obligations. The provision may therefore be excluded or suitably restricted.

Warranties and indemnities

The customer will expect the supplier to give various indemnities and warranties to confirm its levels of commitment. Whether a term of the contract is a condition or a warranty depends on the parties' intentions at the time of

---

2   *Metropolitan Water Board v Dick Kerr and Company* (1918) AC 119.

making the contract. It does not have to be expressly stated as being either one or the other. A warranty is a term of the contract which is less important in principle than a condition. The difference has implications for the remedy available to the innocent party.

A condition is of such primary importance to the contract that if it is not realized, the whole transaction is fundamentally affected. The contract will be repudiated and damages may be claimed by the injured party. An outsourcing contract may have a condition requiring financial guarantees from a parent company or consents from third party licensors to be procured by the supplier by a particular date (there would have to have been some practical reason for the contract to have been executed before obtaining these guarantees or consents). If the condition is not met by the date specified, the contract will be discharged.

Breach of a warranty given by one party will entitle the other party to claim damages under the contract. For example, a supplier may warrant that if its nominated service manager leaves the post, the replacement manager will have similar levels of training, experience and expertise, and the approval of the customer will first be sought. If there is a breach of this warranty and the customer suffers quantifiable loss as a result, a claim for damages may be made.

An indemnity is an express obligation made in the contract to compensate for defined loss or damage, often subject to upper financial limits. For example, the supplier may agree in the contract to indemnify the customer in respect of losses caused by its non-compliance with legislation, infringement of software intellectual property rights as discussed in Chapter 7, damage caused in using the customer's premises, or failure to comply with the exit management plan, as referred to in Chapter 12. The customer may indemnify the supplier in respect of any claim of copyright infringement of its own software and for any losses arising from staff transfer.

Warranties which are not specifically made in the contract will normally be expressly excluded.

Circumscribing performance and limiting liability

The ideal position for the supplier would be a total exclusion of liability arising from any of its activities under the contract.

The ideal position for the customer would be for the supplier to give an indemnity against all the losses and liabilities arising from breach of its obligations under the contract.

Yet it would be unrealistic for any supplier to contract either for no liability or for unlimited liability. The contract will reflect a compromise. The supplier cannot afford to leave itself exposed to compensation for all the customer's losses of whatever kind which it cannot foresee, and for which it is highly unlikely to obtain insurance cover at all, or for which cover is available only at a very high price. The supplier will therefore place an upper financial limit on its liability. If the customer requires additional protection, it may be necessary for it to look to its own insurance, or alternatively to ask the supplier to take out extra cover for which the costs will (at least in part) be passed on to the customer. This is, after all, the last resort. The customer should be confident in its choice of supplier. Through the contract and by means of continuous review and management of the service being provided, the customer should be in a position to arrest most problems at an early stage before they get magnified.

The law prohibits liability being excluded or unreasonably limited under certain conditions. The contract will state that liability causing death or personal injury from negligence will not be excluded or limited. It would not in fact be legitimate to exclude or limit such liability.[3] Similarly, liability arising from negligence for damage to tangible property caused by negligence cannot be excluded, and should therefore be accepted by the supplier, subject to a reasonable limit. These liabilities will be covered under the supplier's public liability insurance. If the contract consists of standard terms of business, liability *cannot* be restricted for breach of contract unless it is 'reasonable' to do so.[4] There is no definition of 'standard terms' in the legislation; a term may be negotiated yet still be regarded as unreasonable if it remains a standard term once agreed.[5] Few outsourcing contracts will be on standard terms. Nevertheless, any outsourcing contract should be fair to both parties.

'Reasonable' is a term now found in much legislation and has to be interpreted in relation to the particular facts. In deciding on whether a contractual term is reasonable in relation to standard terms, the factors taken into account will include the relative bargaining position of the parties; any inducement to agree to the terms; and the availability of insurance to the parties.[6] The overall

---

3   Unfair Contract Terms Act 1977 S2(1).
4   Unfair Contract Terms Act 1977 S3.
5   *St Albans City and District Council v ICL Ltd* (1996) 4 All ER 481.
6   Unfair Contract Terms Act 1977, Schedule 2.

context of the contract will be reviewed if this is necessary to determine what is reasonable.

Further provisions will be a matter for negotiation. The supplier will endeavour to limit its risk, perhaps to a specified sum under its professional indemnity insurance – or to the value of the contract, which the customer should resist. From the customer's point of view, potential losses result from the damage suffered if things go wrong. The risk is not necessarily directly referable to the price being paid.

The supplier ought to be carrying insurance cover for certain events, as an important back up to the contractual relationship. The supplier will never want to find itself in a situation where even if it has failed to carry out its part of the contract, the resulting liability is so great as to wipe out all its profits or even to put it out of business. This will not help the customer either.

It follows that any financial limit of liability specified in the contract should not be arbitrary. It should be justifiable by the supplier – in terms of the type of business, the level of risk to either party, the insurance cover, the value and importance of the contract and the level of the supplier's turnover.[7]

Recoverable losses

The remedy for the party suffering loss is in terms of financial compensation or damages for the direct losses which are foreseeable at the time of entering into the contract. Such losses are those arising in the ordinary course of events from the breach of contract or 'as may reasonably be supposed to be in the contemplation of both parties at the time they made the contract as the probable result of the breach of it'.[8] At the time the contract is made, the supplier and customer will not be expecting any breaches to occur. What is intended by 'contemplation' is that if the breach had been considered as a possibility at the time of entering into the agreement, it would have been concluded that there was a serious likelihood that the loss or damage suffered was likely to arise as a result.

For losses to be recoverable by compensation, they must either arise naturally from the breach of contract or be those which could reasonably be anticipated by both parties to occur if the performance of the contract should fail. Direct damage or loss will be covered but normally other kinds of loss or

---

7   Ibid.
8   *Hadley v Baxendale* (1854) 9 Ex.341, restated and refined in later cases.

damage, described as consequential or indirect, will be categorically excluded in the contract.

What is 'direct' loss or damage? Wasted expenditure has been held to be a direct loss in a case involving a failed computer system.[9] It included support and testing payments, payments to consultants, the cost of wasted computer stationery, and the cost of wasted management time. A shortfall in income and associated interest caused by software error will also be recoverable. On the other hand, loss of data is not normally defined as a direct loss.

Loss of profits would not be directly recoverable unless the customer had drawn to the supplier's attention in advance that this would be a direct result of a failure in the outsourcing arrangements. For a self-contained single system or service outsourced, the losses may be limited. For wholesale outsourcing, if things went wrong, then loss of customer profits would be highly likely to be a direct consequence, particularly if the outsourcing included mission-critical systems. 'Economic' loss is often contractually excluded from the scope of liability. Yet losses suffered by a customer are most likely to be economic. It should be clearly explicit in the contract whether or not loss of profits is to be recoverable if caused by service failure.

One contracting party will not necessarily be fully aware of all the business activities of the other, and of their relative priorities. It is in the customer's interests to advise the supplier during the negotiations of the probable losses which would ensue if the contract were breached. The losses will then be foreseeable in the context of the outsourcing, and the supplier will have been made aware that they matter to the customer.

It is up to the customer to recognize in advance what its financial risks would be if the contract should go wrong, and to communicate these to the supplier. The earlier the contractual process is initiated, the more time the parties will have to consider how best to manage the risks by forward planning as far as possible.

If the matter came to court, judicial discretion might be the arbiter in the decision as to what would be included as the direct losses of the customer for which the supplier would be liable. One commentator said: 'If the judge thinks that justice requires the claimant to be compensated, he will suggest that the loss or damage suffered was likely. If not, he will say that it was too remote'.[10]

---

9   *Salvage Association v CAP Financial Services Limited* (1995) FSR 654.
10   Michael Whinney, in *New Law Journal* 27 March 1992.

Compensation, not penalty

The legal principle under English contract law to compensate for breach of contract is to attempt to put the party not at fault into the position it would have been in if the contract had been carried out properly. It follows that the injured party should not benefit by making a gain which is over and above its actual loss. It is not able to penalize the party at fault, by expecting to receive an arbitrary or an excessive sum of money if the contract is not fulfilled. Any provision in the contract with this objective will not be legally enforceable. Along with this principle is one known as 'mitigation' in that the innocent party is expected to try to mitigate or minimise the loss caused, rather than to take advantage of the situation.

A claim for damages for work badly done would therefore typically be for what it had actually cost to have the work carried out or put right by a third party, but no more than this.

A genuine effort beforehand may be made to estimate certain losses which would arise in the event of a particular breach, and to include this provision in the contract as 'liquidated' damages, meaning the fixed amount which has been calculated. If it is impossible to estimate the potential loss precisely, then the most convincing figure in the circumstances should be agreed of the losses likely to be suffered which would be recoverable at law. Different sums may be set for different breaches. Chapter 4 discusses liquidated damages as a remedy for service level breaches. A liquidated damages provision means that the parties are aware of the extent of liability and their risks under the contract.

If the consequences of the breach make this kind of calculation almost impossible to estimate in advance, some kind of decision has to be taken between the parties for what the customer would be prepared to accept and the supplier willing to concede, which would be acceptable as a bargain made between the parties.

This imposes some limit on what might be payable to the injured party. As far as the actual figures are concerned, if the loss turns out to be less than the estimate, the pre-agreed figure will apply. The parties are regarded at law as free to negotiate and agree a figure to represent liquidated and ascertained damages provided that it does not constitute a penalty. The risk to the customer is that the agreed amount turns out not to be sufficient compensation if the breach of contract and consequent losses are sustained.

However, the supplier's risk is that it would not affect the amount of liquidated damages if at the time of breach of contract, the customer was not in fact suffering any loss, provided that the estimate had been properly calculated. It is therefore important that the customer should be able to justify the reasoning behind any figures. If there were to be an argument, the supplier would immediately be likely to challenge the amount representing the liquidated damages, and to seek to discover how it had been worked out. If the sum had been satisfactorily calculated and agreed in the first place, the supplier's case would be weak.

The amount may be expressed in the contract for purposes of compensation and not intended as a penalty, but if it is in fact a penalty, it does not matter what label it has been given. A single lump sum stated as being payable by way of compensation on the occurrence of one or more or all of several events, with various outcomes of damage, would be presumed to be a penalty. If the liquidated damages figure varies simply by growing in line with the contract value or the supplier's increasing work load, this too would be unlikely on the face of it to be a real estimate in advance. Any amount stated in terms of a percentage of the contract sum runs the risk of not being enforceable. Percentages will give rise to arbitrary figures. It is not obviously logical to relate in this way the value of the contract to potential loss suffered. If the provision were to be held to be a penalty, then the customer would not be deprived of the right to claim for damages, but would have to prove the loss suffered.

Compensation independent of contract

Beyond the contract, one of the parties may be liable in what is known at law as 'tort', a branch of law separate from contract, applying to certain illicit acts, or in some cases omissions, causing damage. One example of a tort is negligence. The party making the claim of negligence, the claimant, would have to prove that the party against whom the claim is made, the defendant, owed it a *duty of care*, a particular legal term for defining the extent of responsibility for the acts in question, that there was a breach of that duty of care, and that the breach caused the damage. The relationship between the claimant and defendant is not automatically going to involve a duty of care. Where it does exist, phrased in legal terms, is where the claimant is so directly and closely affected by the defendant's acts that the defendant should have considered the possibility of harm caused to the claimant.[11] The damages will be measured as the loss caused by the act or default. The defendant will be liable for any loss arising

---

11   *Donoghue v Stevenson* (1932) AC 562.

directly and naturally, which was reasonably foreseeable at the date the act or default happened.

It is possible for liability to exist in tort at the same time as in contract. The fact that the parties have a contract does not in itself prevent there being liability in tort, if this is not excluded under the terms of the contract. For instance there will be an obligation, whether specified in the contract or implied, to take reasonable skill and care in providing the services. There may in any case also be a duty of care to take reasonable skill and care not to be negligent in a broader situation than the scope of the contract itself, perhaps where additional services are carried out.

It would be possible to claim for economic loss independently of the contract as a result of statements made by the defendant, such as loss caused by advice negligently given or misinformation negligently stated, provided that the negligence in making the statement could be proved; that the defendant knew that the statement would be communicated to the claimant; and that the claimant would be relying on it as expert knowledge or professional expertise, for the purposes of entering into the outsourcing arrangements. This might affect either the supplier or the customer.

However, negligent liability other than in contract is subject to some restrictions at law. Claims for economic loss are extremely limited in scope, and it is difficult to predict the situations in which they would have any chance of success. Damages may be recovered in tort for economic loss resulting from negligence only in very narrow circumstances. The defendant must have special knowledge and skill and assume responsibility towards the claimant. The claimant's economic loss must have been caused by negligence of the defendant in misusing the specialist expertise claimed. The claimant must prove reliance on this special knowledge and skill. Normally however, any expectations of expertise between the parties will be expressly set out in the outsourcing contract which will be the source of any legal proceedings.

Commercially, claims in negligence tend to be more expensive to pursue and more difficult technically than claims in contract, and the outcome more uncertain to predict. In a commercial relationship the contract will be the focus. In outsourcing disputes, legal actions based on contract are far more common than actions brought under tort.

Resolving differences

Negotiating a good contract is the best safeguard against disputes developing which cannot be readily sorted out. Terms for dispute prevention should be built into the contract, through controlled procedures for the provision of information, communication, reporting structures and decision making.

Nevertheless, in any close, complex and lasting commercial relationship, differences and disputes are almost inevitable.

Methods for handling disputes should ideally be agreed at the time the contract is being negotiated. Having these techniques set out in the contract itself will save later time, trouble and expense.

Yet no commercially driven agreement of the nature of most outsourcing contracts can anticipate all possible contingencies or be totally unambiguous. Disagreements over what is acceptable, genuine differences of expectations or divergence of opinions are almost inevitable in the performance of complex contracts. Some of the potential difficulties arising have been discussed in earlier chapters. The aim must be to deal with these difficulties before they harden into disputes.

Some arrangements for handling differences of approaches and potential conflicts will be predicated by the particular requirement or service. For example, if software development forms part of the services, this process must have its own checkpoints to allow for variation to the specification as the development is taking place. Change control procedures must allow for assessment of any changes before they are formally agreed and initiated.

Remedies of different levels of magnitude may be sought. The overriding objective is to be able to solve a problem quickly to the mutual satisfaction of the parties, with minimal disruption and costs. This will not always be achievable.

Where there are minor, temporary or single instances of non-compliance with service levels and performance requirements, recompense can be provided for automatically, as discussed earlier in this chapter and in Chapter 4, through a scale of compensation for liquidated damages or service credits associated with payments due, together with action taken to put matters right.

By moving up the decision-making hierarchy, escalation procedures for discussion and problem resolution can be built into the normal management of the contract, as detailed in Chapter 9, to assist in overcoming deadlock. It is often the case that senior managers who are remote from the day-to-day operations will bring a fresh approach to resolving issues.

A final level of escalation procedure within the control of the parties themselves may be contractually provided for by calling an extraordinary management meeting with the aim of resolving differences and maintaining the relationship, to be attended by a small number of named senior representatives of each side.

Another possibility is to bring in an agreed external independent technical expert for determination of certain kinds of disputes of a technical nature – given that the disputing parties can at least agree both on the choice of such a person whose professional verdict they will each accept, and also on what constitutes a dispute confined to technical issues, for example over what should be included in a particular technical definition, or whether a new release of software comprises a new version, upgrade or update, if these are differentially treated in the contract. This can be a relatively quick, informal and flexible way of reaching a decision. The contract wording should be so drafted as to ensure that the expert is appointed to act as an expert, and not as an adjudicator.

Termination is a final sanction. Even here, a last opportunity for negotiations may be a contractual requirement so that the party intending to terminate will have to give a number of days' notification – typically at least one month, expressed as twenty working days – before the termination takes effect. Again this is an opportunity for further discussion and negotiations in the hope of finding a solution to avoid bringing the relationship to an end.

Taking formal action

If the dispute is not resolved by any of the methods discussed above, or if other informal means of negotiation fail, then formal methods of dispute resolution need to be adopted, whether litigation through initiating formal legal court proceedings, Alternative Dispute Resolution ('ADR') or arbitration. If ADR or arbitration is agreed as a suitable forum at the time of negotiating the contract, it should be expressly included as a contractual term.

While formal means of dispute resolution are in progress, the customer may be unwilling to pay the supplier. The contract may set out terms for an interest-bearing bank deposit account to be set up in the names of both parties, so that the customer may continue to comply with its payment obligations, but the sums will be paid into this account. Following resolution of the dispute, the amount in the account, together with accrued interest, can be paid out according to what was determined by the proceedings.

Litigation

Whenever there is a dispute, the parties to a contract may go to court. Legal action must normally be initiated within six years of the date of the breach of contract, or if the breach was fraudulently hidden, six years from when it was discovered. This time limit is known as the limitation period. Some suppliers will argue for this legal right to be restricted contractually to two or three years, on the grounds that this gives a reasonable period of time for formal action to be initiated, makes it more feasible to collate the evidence relating to the breach, and makes their own forward planning and insurance assessment easier. There is normally no reason for the customer to accept this restraint on its legal entitlement unless as a concession in relation to another negotiating point.

For contracts executed as deeds, the limitation period is twelve years. Although it is not necessary for outsourcing contracts to be deeds, some organizations, such as local authorities, have standing orders requiring major contracts to be executed in the form of deeds, and this extended limitation period will be one of the consequences.

To succeed in a civil case in court, the claimant must prove that it has suffered damage caused by the defendant's breach of contract, on the balance of probabilities. Proving and quantifying the breach can be difficult. Over the length of time which litigation may take in progressing from the issue of proceedings to a court hearing, which may extend to a number of years, the parties will have many chances of reaching a settlement. Most cases do in fact settle without a court hearing.

Courts have the powers to compel the production of relevant documents, the attendance of witnesses or join other parties to the action. There are also procedures for relatively speedy summary judgement in situations where there is no real defence to an action.

Under English law, the risks for litigants if a case proceeds to court include an obligation for the loser to pay a large proportion of the winner's legal costs, as well as its own. Litigants will take into account the mounting costs as the litigation proceeds as well as the business case which they are fighting. Costs may exceed the damages being claimed. This can act as an incentive towards settlement.

Alternative dispute resolution while proceedings are continuing is actively encouraged by the courts, as discussed later in this chapter.

Discretionary remedies

It is recognised at law that damages would not inevitably be an appropriate remedy for wrong suffered, where the time span involved from issuing proceedings to the court action in itself would contribute to further wrong.

For example if confidential information had been publicized in breach of a non-disclosure agreement, or if software had been copied in breach of its licence, the damage would have been done. What is required is to prevent the wrongful action being repeated.

An injunction or an order for specific performance is a discretionary remedy which may be ordered at the discretion of the court to stop a breach of contract or to require some positive act to be carried out in accordance with the contract. An interlocutory injunction may be applied for as an emergency remedy before the hearing in court of the full issues relating to the case.

The remedy is 'discretionary' in that the court is not obliged to grant it automatically. In reaching a decision the court will have regard to the state of affairs surrounding the matter. The view may be taken that damages awarded after a full hearing would be adequate compensation and that an injunction is not necessary. The standard of conduct of the parties making the application to the court will be relevant to the court's consideration. If the application was not made promptly or if the applicant was itself also acting wrongfully under the contract, the court would regard this adversely and the application would probably fail.

It is a basic tenet of English justice that an order by the courts should be made only after the defendant has had an opportunity of presenting a case. The exception to this is where it appears that the applicant will suffer injustice because of delay or action by the respondent. An application for an injunction may then be made urgently *ex parte* – which means without the presence at the hearing of the respondent. If this exceptional condition applies, the court will then consider whether any damage might be suffered by the respondent through inability to present its case. An applicant may have to give an undertaking to compensate the respondent if at the full hearing the case were eventually to go against the applicant. The respondent could be compensated for the interim decision under the undertaking given by the applicant. If it is not the case that compensation could be awarded, then the risk of the applicant losing must be outweighed by the risk of injustice to the applicant in deciding on the need for the respondent's presence at the interim hearing. Once the order is made, the respondent should be informed without delay to give the chance of arguing the case at court.

Thus in software piracy, if a respondent knew that an applicant was taking proceedings, there would be a temptation to destroy the evidence by removing the software from the computer system. Urgent action *ex parte* by an applicant may be the only means of getting an effective result.

One extraordinary example of a litigated outsourcing contract where the relationship had broken down and discretionary remedies were claimed was a case between Vertex and Powergen, in 2007.[12] The contract had an estimated value to Vertex of about £30 million the first year, and around £24 million per annum subsequently. The outsourcing was of some of Powergen's customer service activities to Vertex's call centre in India, with a contract term of seven years. Powergen attempted to terminate the contract after one year on the alleged grounds of Vertex's breach of performance obligations.

The case was unusual for two main reasons. The first was because the litigation meant that it was publicized, and parties to outsourcing disputes are usually concerned to maintain confidentiality.

The second reason was that Vertex sought a declaration that Powergen was not entitled to terminate and an injunction to prevent Powergen from stopping Vertex continuing to carry out its contractual obligations – 'specific performance'. This is a remedy sought rarely in the courts and granted even more rarely, in situations where financial compensation could not cover the losses, as discussed earlier. But normally when a commercial relationship has broken down, neither party wants it to be restored by requiring continuing performance. The typical claim is for compensation by way of damages for the breach, and the claimant party would look for a new contract with a new party. But here Vertex claimed that it would be suffering irretrievable and unquantifiable loss. Powergen argued more conventionally that the contract had become unworkable with a failure of co-operation, loss of confidence and

---

12   *Vertex Data Science Limited v Powergen Retail Limited* (2006) EWHC 1340.

mutual distrust. In such circumstances, to require the contract to remain in force was completely unrealistic.

Not surprisingly the Court found that the contract required extensive mutual co-operation, and that this was not going to happen. It refused to compel Powergen to keep working with Vertex. The judge referred to the complexity and length of the contract, even though in places it was not sufficiently detailed concerning the respective responsibilities of the parties. These characteristics are not untypical of outsourcing contracts.

Alternative Dispute Resolution

Alternative Dispute Resolution ('ADR') is an umbrella term for an approach formalising concepts of mediation and conciliation. It stresses each party's own responsibility for voluntary negotiation for the purpose of settling disputes in a non-binding context. It is used as an adjudication process in itself as an alternative to litigation, or it can be brought in at any stage during litigation. The process can be halted without further obligation or commitment at the behest of either party. Even if the mediation is not successful in the ultimate resolution of the dispute, it may reduce the number or the complexity of the issues concerned. There are a number of ADR options which can be modified as required by the parties, and which range from informal conciliation to consideration of the issues in a mini-trial format by a third party. The basis is that an independent neutral third party will be appointed by or on behalf of the parties in dispute, who will not be a decision-making adjudicator, but a facilitator acting with the active consent of both parties, trained to guide the parties themselves to reach a negotiated and perhaps creative compromise. Experts may participate. It is important to a successful outcome that the facilitator is skilled and able to avoid any appearance of bias, and also understands the business context and the nature of the problems.

It is also important that the representatives of the parties who are involved in the process have authority to settle on behalf of their organizations.

Because ADR is voluntary, the parties do not have to agree in advance to be bound by the outcome; in fact it may be explicitly stated that they do not need so to agree.

If the parties wish to include ADR in the contract as the first formal means of trying to resolve a dispute, the position about costs should be clarified, for example that each party will bear its own costs incurred in taking part and equally share the facilitator's costs. A time limit may be contractually imposed so as to avoid ADR being misused as a delaying tactic.

Information gained in the course of the mediation, such as weaknesses which are learned about the other party's case, could be exploited in subsequent litigation, if the ADR is not successful. A mediator will normally be required not to pass on confidential information, as part of the ADR instructions. There should also be a provision that the negotiations themselves should be conducted in confidence without prejudice to the parties' rights in legal proceedings. The parties may thereby have to agree not to introduce certain material revealed by the ADR procedures into judicial proceedings, for instance any opinions about the basis for the settlement facilitated by the conciliator or mediator. Reference to a failed ADR process conducted on a formal 'without prejudice' basis will not be permitted in subsequent litigation. Care must be taken in drafting the ADR clauses, to ensure that the implications are covered and understood.

The English courts are now required to promote the use of ADR in appropriate cases of litigation and to facilitate it through case management. The Mediation Directive[13] reinforces this by promoting the voluntary use of mediation for cross-border commercial disputes in the EU as an alternative to judicial proceedings, with the objective of achieving better access to justice – and the amicable settlement of disputes. It encourages courts to refer parties to mediation. Procedurally it enables settlements resulting from mediation to be enforceable in the courts, and provides protection for mediators normally from being called as witnesses. It states that mediation must be confidential – so that information discovered by one party against the other during mediation cannot be used against that party subsequently in litigation if the mediation fails. It also requires member states to encourage the development of voluntary codes of conduct, and other quality control mechanisms, and mediator training.

Although the English courts will not inevitably require the parties to mediate, they expect the parties to consider whether ADR would be appropriate. The litigation timetable may be halted while the parties try and settle the dispute through ADR. There may be costs sanctions against a successful party who has refused to use ADR, and thereby caused increased delay, costs and effort in resolving the case.[14] Factors which the court will take into account will include the subject matter, the costs of mediating, any risks of delaying trial and the merits of the case. In one case the defendant had correctly maintained that its

---

13 Directive 2008/52/EC on certain aspects of mediation in civil and commercial matters.
14 *Dunnett v Railtrack plc* (in administration) (2002) EWCA Civ 303; [2002] All ER 850.

prospects of success in the litigation were high. There was no costs penalty in this case.[15]

In a world-wide IT outsourcing services agreement between Cable & Wireless and IBM,[16] there was a clause providing for dispute resolution to be attempted through ADR procedures, as recommended by the Centre for Dispute Resolution. When a dispute arose, Cable & Wireless commenced legal proceedings, claiming that the clause was merely an '"agreement to negotiate" and too vague to be enforceable.'

The normal principle is that only contractual provisions which are definite in what they say will be upheld by the courts. Agreements to negotiate will not be enforceable because they lack certainty and are impracticable. Yet it was held by the court in this case that it would 'fly in the face of public policy' not to enforce an unqualified reference to ADR. There simply had to be an obligation to mediate 'expressed in unqualified and mandatory terms'. The parties were required to work through the ADR procedure.

ADR is certainly worth considering where both parties appreciate that a continuation of their working relationship is desirable: where there are points in favour of each side's case, where the underlying business interests of each party are clear, where each party is genuinely ready to listen to the other side of the argument, and where both parties are clear that they wish to avoid high costs of litigation or arbitration. Its value lies in the chance of achieving an early settlement cheaply by responsiveness to the parties' needs. Although it may be used at any stage of a dispute, and as an adjunct during the course of litigation or arbitration, if there are ADR provisions in the contract, then that procedure must first be followed before initiating legal proceedings through the courts. If the parties agree on this route, one good reason for putting it in the contract is to avoid any appearance to the other party of weakness by suggesting it at the time the dispute arises. Sometimes a practical solution which is beyond the powers of the courts to achieve, but which may be more readily brought about through ADR, will be a useful result for the parties rather than a legal ruling.

However, ADR is not automatically the best route to follow. More information may be disclosed to the other party than is wise, especially if the process is unsuccessful and proceedings are issued. In certain instances, such as alleged fraud, or where there are novel or important points of law, ADR will not be appropriate, since the courts have the relevant experience. Cases concerned

15 Hurst v Leeming (2002) EWHC 1051 (Ch).
16 *Cable & Wireless plc v IBM United Kingdom Limited* [2002] 2 All ER (Comm) 1041.

with legal principles will still require legal adjudication processes. The success of certain remedies at law, such as injunctions which were discussed earlier in this chapter, may be inhibited if action is not taken early because ADR was tried and failed. A settlement agreed through the ADR process is not so easily enforceable as a court judgment – and a settlement may not even be reached.

Nevertheless ADR is becoming integral to litigation and the overall dispute resolution context.

Arbitration

Since the beginning of the 20th century, arbitration has been a major method of formal dispute resolution. Arbitration is an adversarial process with an impartial arbitrator, or possibly more than one arbitrator in highly complex and high value disputes, who will adjudicate by making a decision or an award. An arbitrator must be selected who is acceptable to both sides, with expertise concerning the area in dispute, and sound knowledge about arbitration procedures.

Arbitrators' powers depend on the legal jurisdiction and the procedural rules of the parties. In the UK, the Arbitration Act[17] sets out the scope of arbitration proceedings and the powers of the arbitrator. It is based on the principles of resolving disputes impartially, avoiding delay and expense as far as possible, providing essential safeguards, and autonomy for the parties in making choices about the methods to be adopted. There is a framework of formal rules, but the procedures are more adaptable than in litigation because the arbitration tribunal is appointed to deal with a single dispute. The few mandatory provisions are limited to such matters as the enforcement of a ruling or an award made by the arbitrator. Otherwise the parties are free to make their own arrangements for conducting the arbitration. If there is no agreement about procedure made between the parties, the arbitrator is given wide powers to decide on the conduct of the arbitration, evidence and procedure.

The scope of arbitration therefore lies within the control of the parties. Terms should be set out in advance in the contract, to make arbitation mandatory if there is a dispute, define where the arbitration is to be held, the number of arbitrators, the governing law, rules of evidence and formalities of procedure which will apply. The parties can control the the timing of the hearing. Whereas a case listed for hearing in court will have to join the queue for a date which may

---

17   Arbitration Act 1996.

be months or years ahead, an arbitrator or a team of arbitrators can be appointed who do not have a backlog of cases to deal with or other commitments, and who will be available within a short space of time.

A decision made by the arbitrator will be final and binding on the parties, and cannot be appealed, unless it can be shown to be wrong in law or that the arbitrator acted in bad faith.

Arbitration proceedings take place in private. There are occasions where publicity is a useful lever in negotiating a dispute – for either party. However, the confidentiality of the process may assist the parties in continuing to trade, if there has been no denigration in public and reputations have not been lost.

Arbitration should not be accepted automatically as a means of dispute resolution without realising the implications in relation to costs, lack of publicity and choice of arbitrator. The arbitrator's fees must be paid, and even if the matter settles beforehand, the arbitrator may nevertheless be entitled to some payment. A neutral location for the arbitration proceedings must be found and paid for.

An arbitrator has no power to bring in a party who was not party to the original agreement to arbitrate without their consent. If other parties are likely to be involved, litigation will be a more practical means of dispute resolution.

Choosing an arbitrator or mediator

A designated organization can be appointed in the contract in order to select an arbitrator or mediator if the parties cannot agree on a suitable person within a given number of days or do not know of one. Appropriate bodies would be the British Computer Society, the Society for Computers and Law or the Law Society. The Chartered Institute of Arbitrators is the UK's professional organization for arbitrators, which also deals in mediation. The Centre for Dispute Resolution, known as 'CEDR', is one of a number of independent organizations set up to handle disputes which fall to be resolved through ADR. Its scheme for IT disputes is linked with the trade body Intellect. Another is the ADR Group. The addresses of these organizations are set out in Chapter 15.

Offshore Outsourcing CHAPTER 14

Offshoring is about moving work abroad, largely for labour cost savings reasons. There are now many outsourcing contracts offshore. A wide range of IT services is outsourced, of varying levels of complexity and sophistication. Call centre services are popular and at the other end of the spectrum, business process outsourcing services are also successfully outsourced. 'Nearshoring' is a term sometimes used for outsourcing to countries nearer home, but the discussion in this chapter covers issues affecting outsourcing to any country abroad.

Technological advances, particularly in telecommunications, have enabled services to be provided remotely yet seamlessly. The market for offshore outsourcing has developed in certain countries where the infrastructure is sufficiently developed (for example, internet bandwidth and tele-communications networks) and importantly where labour costs are lower, even for highly skilled staff who speak English, and staff turnover is low. Although there are additional costs in negotiating the arrangements and entering into the contract, overall there are significant costs savings.

India has been a preferred location, steadily increasing in popularity since the 1980s. However, other countries in the Far East are increasing market share, and Russia and countries in Eastern Europe have also become major players. Offshore countries are now focusing on different niche markets. Warnings are emerging that the growing demand for local expertise may lead to rising labour costs for certain locations continually expanding for outsourcing arrangements.

There are many IT services and circumstances for which offshoring is not a realistic option. Being physically on-site or nearby is often essential. Local employee flexibility may be another consideration. Potential costs reductions may be insignificant compared with the value of controlling the service activity in close proximity. In the public sector, political considerations may require outsourcing to remain local.

There are a number of issues which will need extensive evaluation and assessment for the offshore outsourcing contract.

Impact of globalization

Economists are convinced that free trade is beneficial and that international competition leads to increased productivity, more effective use of new technology and innovation. In any event it is not possible to stem the global trade in IT services.

However, there is a perception that jobs are lost through offshoring. The evidence currently available suggests that this is not the case for service industries, but that this becomes evident only in the medium and long term. The Organization for Economic Co-operation and Development (OECD),[1] founded in 1961, with some thirty countries in membership, provides reliable reports, statistics and data as part of its purpose of enabling democratic governments to work together to promote economic growth and financial stability, to increase world trade and to communicate with other countries about these issues. It monitors trends, makes analyses and forecasts, and carries out research in areas of trade, technology, taxation and so on.

OECD has published a number of papers on various aspects of offshoring, based on statistical and survey material. One report[2] found that offshoring was not a major cause of job losses in the service sector. Indeed, companies which had successfully transferred services offshore improved their competitive position, which could lead to job creation in their countries. Bankruptcies and restructurings were far greater causes of job losses. The public perception of job losses in the service sector through offshoring is not borne out by the economic evidence for the medium term, although it is hard to quantify.

The World Trade Organization, WTO,[3] is a forum for governments to negotiate trade agreements, and an organization for liberalising trade. It also has reported on offshoring. Its 2005 annual *World Trade Report* maintained that the threats for domestic employment from offshoring were exaggerated, and not supported by the facts. Another report, two years later, jointly with

---

1   http://www.oecd.org.
2   Offshoring and Employment: Trends and Impacts, 2007.
3   http://www.wto.org.

the International Labour Office, said that the dynamic situation of trade and offshoring made it difficult to predict in the short term which jobs were at risk or in demand.

However, a report published in 2007[4] jointly by the International Labour Office and the WTO Secretariat, said that the changing nature of trade and in particular the role of offshoring is likely to make it increasingly difficult for policymakers to predict which jobs are at risk and which jobs will be in demand in the near future.

Certainly the unions are concerned. Unite[5] is the largest union in the United Kingdom, with over two million members in both manufacturing and service industries. It recognises that offshoring is going to continue. It is frequently involved in negotiations relating to offshoring on behalf of its members. It wants the Government to develop a best practice benchmark so that companies proposing to offshore take into account the likely impact on employees both in the UK and abroad.

Major example

At one end of the spectrum as an offshore outsourcing customer is E I Dupont de Nemours & Co. This company operates in seventy countries and various markets. In 1997 it entered into world-wide outsourcing agreements and strategic alliance agreements with Computer Sciences Corporation and Andersen Consulting LLP at a value of $4 billion over ten years.[6] This agreement remains one of the biggest and most innovative of its kind. The company wanted to undertake a business transformation in the forty countries where it worked, which would be supported and managed by IT services with flexibility, yet at the same time it expected to contain its costs, increase its productivity and efficiency: no small wish list. The outsourcing covered telecommunications and IT services, including both operations and applications. 2,600 employees transferred. The success of the contract may be perceived by the fact that it was extended for seven years in 2005, with an estimated value of $2 billion, covering IT infrastructure and applications world-wide.

For an offshore IT outsourcing contract, certain provisions will need additional attention. For the selection of the supplier, the structure of the arrangements, the location and the jurisdiction must be evaluated.

---

4 *Trade and Employment: Challenges for Policy Research.*
5 http://www.unitetheunion.org.
6 http://www.csc.com/industries/chemicalenergynaturalresources/casestudies/4149.shtml.

Structure

The typical offshore IT outsourcing is with a supplier based abroad. There are variations to this model.

One option is to enter into the contract with an UK supplier established onshore which has an offshore subsidiary. The onshore supplier can then act as the intermediary, and may be responsible for the insurances covering liability under the agreement. Enforcing a judgement if the onshore company has assets is easier than enforcing a judgment against an offshore company. A contract with an established UK supplier may make it less apparent for the customer's public relations purposes that it has entered into an offshore outsourcing arrangement, particularly if the services being outsourced are not front-line services, such as call centres. Public sector offshore IT outsourcing arrangements may take this route.

A recent alternative to offshore IT outsourcing is the expansion of a company's own operations into a foreign country with lower labour costs by setting up 'captive' facilities there, with its own offices and employing staff directly.

In any event, in selecting the supplier, the customer must ensure that the entity has assets and revenue streams as back up for its obligations.

Location

Additional factors to consider in relation to the choice of location are whether there are any risks of natural disasters from the geographical situation. The political stability of the region and the local government's attitude to outsourcing will be highly relevant. There may be tax incentives, or alternatively tax implications may need to be factored into the financial calculations. How the services, payments and even the corporate vehicle itself are structured may be very important for this. Advice from specialist lawyers and other advisers in the jurisdiction is essential.

Time differences may be relevant, for example, for call centre services.

Offshore IT services contracts may be an exception to the general principle of excluding force majeure from the contract as discussed in Chapter 13. It may well be the case that force majeure should operate to cover the possibility of political or natural disasters. However, a simple right to suspend or terminate will not help the customer, and the potential circumstances need to be carefully evaluated as to the most effective solution if any such problems were to arise.

Contract jurisdiction and international disputes

Basic advice on contract jurisdiction was given in Chapter 1. The parties should expressly agree in the contract which jurisdiction applies for the construction of the contract wording and in case of any disputes, which legal forum should prevail. In the unfortunate event that there is no such agreement, where one of the parties to the contract is not a company registered in the UK, normally the starting point for the legal jurisdiction applicable would be basically that with which the organization contract is most closely connected.

For an English or Welsh company which is party to the contract the preference would be for the law of England and Wales to govern the contract provisions, to apply to the meaning of the contract wording and its construction, or for jurisdiction in the event of a dispute.[7] The assumption as to the most appropriate legal system will need to be reviewed in the light of tax or other advice relating to the advantages of offshoring.

In the unfortunate event that there is no such express agreement, normally the starting point for the legal jurisdiction applicable would be that with which the contract is most closely connected. This would need to be examined at the time of the dispute, and there is no substitute for the convenience of explicit contractual agreement

For disputes, a robust escalation procedure in the contract, as discussed in Chapter 10, is essential.

The City of London is one of the world's principal financial and commercial centres. The wide use of the English language in IT and in international business is an advantage. A majority of the cases in the Commercial Court, which handles complex trade and commercial cases, have an international dimension, where one or all the parties may not be based in the UK.

Arbitration is discussed in Chapter 13. London is world-famous as a first class commercial arbitration centre. For international arbitration, the principal established bodies are the London Court of International Arbitration, and also the International Court of Arbitration based in Paris, and the American

---

7   Rome Convention 1980, revised by the EU's Rome I Regulation.

Arbitration Association. The addresses for these organizations are set out in Chapter 15. Binding arbitration is often a practical formal dispute resolution mechanism for international contracts and therefore for offshore outsourcing.

Note that once there is a decision from an arbitrator or from a court, the courts in the supplier's country must enter a judgement in favour of that decision in order for it to be enforceable there. Sometimes this is simply not possible. In other instances it can continue to take several years for courts of certain other countries to hear proceedings based on the judgment of a foreign court when necessary to enforce it. It is often advisable to select a neutral foreign venue for arbitration. It usually takes less time to enforce foreign arbitral awards made under international arbitration regimes. Recovery of money may be more difficult, and various approaches may be considered to allow for this, such as an escrow account for money to be released only on specific trigger events. Other factors which call for increased vigilance, time and effort in negotiating the contract include charging arrangements, offshore labour considerations, data protection and security generally, and intellectual property protection.

Charges

Although cost reduction is one of the main reasons for offshoring contracts, various significant additional expenses and costs will arise, both one-off and continuing, which must be taken into account.

Choosing an offshore supplier and negotiating the agreement will be far more expensive than the costs of entering into a contract with a supplier based in the same jurisdiction. Investigating the cultural aspects, the local laws and the provider's financial and corporate status, assessing any taxation and other financial incentives, carrying out the due diligence, will all take considerable effort, time and expense. There will be increased transition management costs at the outset, and increased service management costs throughout the contract life. There will be currency risks and fluctuations and possibly exchange control issues. Onshore personnel will visit the offshore location, perhaps for weeks or even months at a time. Offshore staff will visit the workplace onshore and likewise may work there for weeks or months.

The costs – and risks – increase when a company has multiple offices in different locations and countries, depending on the degree of decentralized decision making and autonomy of local offices. It may be that the rationale for outsourcing will enable service functions and processes spread over many sites to be centralized.

Offshore labour

Local labour costs will be a major factor in the customer's decision-making process.

The host country's laws must be reviewed in relation to the contract, not least its local employment legislation. There are many potential legal risks in relation to employees, with ramifications for the contract, depending on where the offshoring is to be and the laws and regulations applying to local and foreign workers. The customer's domestic employees may need to visit or work at the offshore location occasionally, and certain managers working offshore will certainly need to spend time with the customer's operations at the home location from time to time.

What staff training and development, both initially and ongoing, will be necessary, and how will it be carried out and how often?

Do the outsourcing staff need to understand the customer's business and culture, or the customer's end user style? It may be necessary to describe the services and assess the service levels with great precision for the contract. Cultural differences in formality, assumptions, communication, meanings and styles must be allowed for and managed. There are specialised consultancies who advise specifically on cultural issues relating to offshore outsourcing.

TUPE rules as discussed in Chapter 6 apply to offshoring work too. If there is a transfer of a business situated in the UK immediately before the transfer, then TUPE will apply. It will operate so as to transfer to the outsourcing supplier the contracts of employment and the liabilities of the employer under those employment contracts. So here too specialist legal advice will apply on how to manage this effectively. However, TUPE will not apply when the contract comes to an end, because the transferor will not be situated in the UK immediately before the transfer.

What is likely to happen is that even if TUPE applies, an automatic transfer of employment to the external service provider, with preservation of existing employment benefits, is not going to benefit workers in the UK who are in general hardly likely to want to move to the offshore location. There are more likely to be redundancies. TUPE and the contract will determine who pays for the cost of these. The UK company will pay direct or indemnify the offshore supplier.

Data protection and security

The terms for data protection are defined and the purposes of data protection are discussed in Chapter 11. The further considerations which apply for transferring employees' personal data offshore form part of that discussion. The eighth data protection principle states that the customer must not transfer personal data to countries without adequate protection unless the data subject has given consent or unless other specific exceptions are satisfied. This effectively imposes EU data protection standards in jurisdictions outside Europe. The Information Commissioner's website[8] has various guidance notes in relation to data protection and offshore outsourcing.

Security is important wherever the supplier is based. If the outsourcing involves extensive electronic communication and networking online, this must be made very secure. There may be specific laws in the offshore environment, which should be accounted for in the contract but also reinforced with special policies and practices for the offshoring staff to follow.

Intellectual property rights

To supplement the advice given in Chapter 7 about intellectual property rights, it is worth considering whether the offshore jurisdiction has signed up to the WTO's TRIPS agreement or other international agreements.

WTO is the World Trade Organization.[9] TRIPS is the Agreement on Trade-related Aspects of Intellectual Property Rights[10] which covers all aspects of intellectual property in one multilateral agreement, requiring signatories to have basic standards of intellectual property protection. The Agreement provides for substantive rules, procedure and enforcement. Its stated purpose is to improve worldwide protection of intellectual property and to foster international creativity and technology transfer.

The TRIPS Agreement is one of the three pillars of the WTO system. The others are the revised GATT (the General Agreement on Tariffs and Trade), covering rules for international trade in goods and GATS (General Agreement on Trade in Services). The WTO has a dispute settlement mechanism for settling disputes concerning rights and obligations under the Agreement.

---

8   http://www.ico.gov.uk.
9   http://www.wto.org.
10   http://www.wto.org/english/tratop_e/trips_e/trips_e.htm.

Contract management

Time must be invested by the customer with the offshore staff before the contract is entered into. Once the contract is signed, continuity of management liaison is even more important in a situation where supplier and customer are in countries distant from each other. The extent of face-to-face meetings and whether sometimes staff from one country may be required to work in the other location for a time must be agreed.

Termination/expiry

On expiry or termination of an offshore outsourcing, the loss of knowledge and expertise may have more severe repercussions than in a domestic outsourcing, and it may be harder to recover the services.

The Financial Services Authority provides guidance on outsourcing, covering some of the issues discussed in this chapter, particularly management structures, business continuity arrangements and audit provisions.[11] One report on industry practices for offshore operations[12] reminds directors and senior managers that they are responsible for assessing and managing risks including those relating to outsourcing and offshoring. The document states that offshoring is no more risky than domestic outsourcing provided that there is suitable risk monitoring. It expects regulated firms to deal with operational risks arising from offshoring, and provides examples of good practice of monitoring and managing risks.

The trends at present for offshore outsourcing are towards a variety of corporate arrangements, not simply a direct relationship between the external service provider and the customer. The number of offshore IT outsourcing contracts continues to grow, with the development of innovative forms of relationships, although as more selective outsourcing takes place, the average individual contract value is not increasing at the same rate.

---

11 http://www.fsa.gov.uk.
12 Financial Services Authority, *Offshore Operations; Industry Feedback*, 2005 http://www.fsa.gov.uk/pubs/other/offshore_ops.pdf.

Conclusion

CHAPTER 15

In conclusion then, here are some of the main points to watch out for in the outsourcing contract. One possible structure of headings for the services agreement and the business transfer, together with the schedules which may be needed is proposed, which may serve as a check list and reminder of the issues which have to be addressed.

So, what are the main lessons to be learned? First and foremost a customer's existing IT problem will not be successfully solved merely by outsourcing. Certainly there are outsourcing suppliers who will be willing and capable of taking over a customer's IT facilities and services in an unsatisfactory state and improving them. This will be an effective means of overcoming the problems within contained costings only where the customer is making a positive contribution in planning for and creating the contract, and in having ongoing review processes in place. The customer must retain control of the strategic direction of the contract. If there are no suitable internal resources, this control may have to be achieved by buying in consultancy expertise from a source with no interest in providing any prospective outsourcing service itself.

Lack of preparatory work by the customer and the imposition of an unrealistically short timetable will not provide the ground work for a successful outsourcing contract. A customer/supplier mismatch is less likely to occur if the customer's preliminary investigations into its outsourcing requirements and searches for the appropriate supplier have been carried out wisely. As with any system procurement, badly defined service requirements cause hidden costs. A supplier who does not understand the customer's business will not provide the service required.

Customers will be more likely to select the best supplier for what they want and to negotiate a successful outsourcing contract if they are aware of their priorities: whether these are primarily a focus on the core business; better utilization of in-house staff; flexibility of IT response; better quality service; or cost savings above everything else.

Outsourcing is characteristically selective rather than wholesale, taking on average a quarter of a company's IT budget. Selective outsourcing is more likely to meet a customer's expectations and will carry less risk than total outsourcing. The wholesale outsourcings that are so newsworthy are actually atypical.

The contract should be clear and understandable, and ideally will be a pragmatic working document, setting out the details of the particular arrangements. Through the drafting and negotiating of acceptable terms, it is the principal means of managing the legal risks in outsourcing, and once it has been executed, in managing, monitoring and measuring the services. It facilitates the business planning and implementation for balancing the rights and responsibilities of both parties so that they can work together.

Thus the ground must be prepared, the supplier selected, the staff issues managed. If, in spite of this, the outsourcing becomes an outright failure, the terms of the contract must be enforced, by termination if necessary, and alternative arrangements made.

Contract structure

Here is one suggested format for the Services Agreement and the Business Transfer Agreement.

SERVICES AGREEMENT

Introductory provisions

- The Parties:

    Names and addresses of the customer and the outsourcing provider.

- Recitals:

    A brief note on the purposes and background of the Agreement, conventionally set out in two or three paragraphs.

- Execution:

    The signatures of the parties may appear here or at the end of the Agreement.

- Definitions used in the contract

Commercial provisions

- Duration of Contract
- Services – preparatory services if appropriate
- Requirements to meet Service Levels
- Supplier Responsibilities
- Customer Responsibilities
- Charging Provisions and Payment Terms
- Accommodation
- Intellectual Property and Software Licensing
- Management Control and Representatives
- Key Employees
- Change Control
- Contract Variations

Security

- Confidentiality
- Publicity and Public Announcements
- Audit Requirements
- Contingency Planning and Disaster Recovery

Levels of risk

- Warranties
- Indemnities and Limits of Liability
- Liquidated Damages

Termination

- Termination for Cause
- Effects of Termination
- Assistance on Termination

- Exit Management Plan

General provisions, including:

- Entire Agreement:

  What has been agreed, not extraneous documents or verbal agreements.

- Assignment:

  Whether assignment to another party is permissible.

- Severability:

  If one provision is ineffective, this will not affect the remaining terms.

- Waiver:

  If a breach is not enforced at any time, this does not affect its subsequent enforceability.

- Notices:

  Formal notices to be in writing and provisions as to acceptability.

- Governing Law and Dispute Resolution procedures

SERVICES AGREEMENT: ATTACHED CONTRACTS AND SCHEDULES AND AGREEMENTS

- Business Transfer Agreement
- Scope of Services
- Service Level Agreements
- Hardware details
- Software details
- Staff details
- Charges details
- Management Liaison details
- Client Policies
- Disaster Recovery Provisions

BUSINESS TRANSFER AGREEMENT

- Definitions and Interpretations
- Sale and Purchase
- Assets Included in the Transfer
- Taxes
- Completion
- Apportionments and Pre-payments
- Conduct between Commencement Date and Cutover
- Employees
- Third Party Contracts
- Warranties
- Costs and Stamp Duty
- Further Assurance and Assistance
- Confidential Information
- Limits on Liability
- Access to Retained Records and Assistance with Disputes
- Announcements and Publicity

General provisions (see Services Agreement format) including:

- Entire Agreement
- Assignment
- Severability
- Waiver
- Notices
- Governing Law and Dispute Resolution

BUSINESS TRANSFER AGREEMENT: ATTACHED CONTRACTS AND SCHEDULES AND AGREEMENTS

- Assets
- Employment Details

- Property Agreements

- Third Party Contracts

- Pensions

Addresses of organizations mentioned

Academy of Experts
3 Gray's Inn Square
London WC1R 5AH
Tel: +44 (0) 20 7430 0333
email: admin@academy-experts.org
http://www.academy-experts.org

Advisory, Conciliation and Arbitration Service (ACAS)
The Cube
123 Albion Street
Leeds LS2 8ER
Tel: 08457 47 47 47
http://www.acas.org.uk

ADR Group
Grove House
Grove Road
Redland
Bristol BS6 6UN
Tel: +44 (0) 117 946 7180
email: info@adrgroup.co.uk
http://www.adrgroup.co.uk

American Arbitration Association
1633 Broadway
10th Floor
New York 10019
Tel: 001-800-778-7879
http://www.adrgroup.org

The British Computer Society (BCS)
First Floor, Block D
North Star House
North Star Avenue
Swindon SN2 1FA
Tel: +44 (0) 1793 417417
http://www.bcs.org

The British Standards Institution
BSI British Standards
389 Chiswick High Road
London W4 4AL
Tel: +44 (0) 20 8996 9001
email: cservices@bsigroup.com
http://www.bsigroup.com

Centre for Effective Dispute Resolution (CEDR)
International Dispute Resolution Centre
70 Fleet Street
London EC4Y 1EU
Tel: +44 (0) 20 7536 6000
email: info@cedr.com
http://www.cedr.co.uk

The Chartered Institute of Arbitrators
International Arbitration and Mediation Centre
12 Bloomsbury Square
London WC1A 2LP
Tel: +44 (0) 20 7421 7444
email: info@arbitrators.org
http://www.arbitrators.org

Office of the European Commission (Brussels)
Commission of the European Community
200 Rue de la Loi
B-1049 Brussels
Belgium
Tel: 0032 2 235 1111

Office of the European Commission (UK)

England
Jean Monnet House
8 Storeys Gate
London SW1P 3AT
Tel: +44 (0) 20 7973 1992

Scotland
The Tun
4 Jackson's Entry
Holyrood Road
Edinburgh EH8 8PJ
Tel: +44 (0) 131 557 7866

Wales
2 Caspian Point
Caspian Way
Cardiff CF10 4QQ
Tel: +44 (0) 29 2089 5020

Northern Ireland
Windsor House
9/15 Bedford Street
Belfast BT2 7EG
Tel: +44 (0) 28 9024 0708

European Parliament Information Office (UK)
2 Queen Anne's Gate
London SW1A 9AA
Tel: +44 (0) 20 7227 4300

Europe Direct
This service provides information and advice about citizens' rights in the
European Union.
Tel: 0800 6789 1011
http://www.europa.eu.int/europedirect

Main office in Brussels
Rue de la Loi 200
B-1049 Brussels
Tel: 0032 2295 1111
Fax: 0032 22950281

Computer Economics, Inc.
2082 Business Center Dr. Ste 240
Irvine CA 92612
http://www.computereconomics.com

Computer Weekly **magazine**
Quadrant House
The Quadrant
Sutton
Surrey SM2 5AS
http://www.computerweekly.com

Computing **magazine**
Incisive Media Limited,
Haymarket House
28–29 Haymarket
London SW1Y 4RX
http://www.computing.co.uk/

Financial Services Authority
25 The North Colonnade
Canary Wharf
London E14 5HS
Tel: +44 (0) 20 7066 1000
http://www.fsa.gov.uk

The Information Commissioner's Office
Springfield House
Water Lane
Wilmslow
Cheshire SK9 5AK
Tel: 08456 30 60 60
01625 54 57 45
http://www.ico.gov.uk/

The Institute of Internal Auditors - UK and Ireland Ltd
13 Abbeville Mews
88 Clapham Park Road
London SW4 7BX
Tel: +44 (0) 20 7498 0101
http://www.iia.org.uk

Institute for the Management of Information Systems (IMIS)
5 Kingfisher House
New Mill Road
Orpington
Kent BR5 3QG
Tel: +44 (0) 700 00 23456
email: central@imis.org.uk
http://www.imis.org.uk/contact

Intellect
Russell Square House
10–12 Russell Square
London WC1B 5EE
Tel: +44 (0) 20 7331 2000
http://www.intellectuk.org

International Court of Arbitration
Secretariat of the ICC International Court of Arbitration
38 cours Albert 1er
75008 Paris, France
Tel: +33 1 49 53 29 05
http://www.iccwbo.org/court

The Law Society of England and Wales
The Law Society's Hall
113 Chancery Lane
London WC2A 1PL
Tel: +44 (0) 20 7242 1222
email: contact@lawsociety.org.uk
http://www.lawsociety.org.uk/offices/locations.page

London Court of International Arbitration (LCIA)
70 Fleet Street
London EC4Y 1EU
Tel: +44 (0) 20 7936 7007
email: lcia@lcia.org
http://www.lcia-arbitration.com

National Computing Centre (NCC)
Oxford House
Oxford Road
Manchester M1 7ED
Tel: +44 (0) 161 228 6333
email: info@ncc.co.uk
http://www.ncc.co.uk

Society for Computers and Law (SCL)
10 Hurle Crescent
Clifton
Bristol BS8 2TA
Tel: +44 (0) 117 923 7393
http://www.scl.org

Unite the Union
General Secretary
35 King Street
Covent Garden
London WC2E 8JG
http://www.unitetheunion.org.uk

World Trad Organization
Centre William Rappard
Rue de Lausanne 154
CH-1211 Geneva 21
Switzerland
Tel: 0041 22 739 51 11
email: enquiries@wto.org
http://www.wto.org

Index

If you have found this book useful you may be interested in other titles from Gower

The Bid Manager's Handbook
David Nickson
Hardback: 978-0-566-08847-6

The Contract Scorecard:
Successful Outsourcing by Design
Sara Cullen
Hardback: 978-0-566-08793-6
e-book: 978-0-7546-8171-7

Law for Project Managers
David Wright
Hardback: 978-0-566-08601-4

Project Reviews, Assurance and Governance
Graham Oakes
Hardback: 978-0-566-08807-0
e-book: 978-0-7546-8146-5

Purchasing Performance:
Measuring, Marketing and Selling the Purchasing Function
Derek Roylance
Hardback: 978-0-566-08678-6
e-book: 978-0-7546-8308-7

GOWER

The Relationship Manager:
The Next Generation of Project Management
Tony Davis and Richard Pharro
Hardback: 978-0-566-08463-8

Shared Services in Finance and Accounting
Tom Olavi Bangemann
Hardback: 978-0-566-08607-6

Strategic Negotiation
Gavin Kennedy
Hardback: 978-0-566-08797-4

Tools for Complex Projects
Kaye Remington and Julien Pollack
Hardback: 978-0-566-08741-7

Winning New Business in Construction
Terry Gillen
Hardback: 978-0-566-08615-1
e-book: 978-0-7546-8549-4

Visit **www.gowerpublishing.com** and

- search the entire catalogue of Gower books in print
- order titles online at 10% discount
- take advantage of special offers
- sign up for our monthly e-mail update service
- download free sample chapters from all recent titles
- download or order our catalogue